LIBRARY CLASSIFICATION AND BROWSING
THE CONJUNCTION OF READERS AND DOCUMENTS

To Yaacov
with love

LIBRARY CLASSIFICATION AND BROWSING

THE CONJUCTION OF READERS AND DOCUMENTS

Snunith Shoham

sussex
ACADEMIC
PRESS

BRIGHTON • PORTLAND

2 4 6 8 10 9 7 5 3 1
First published 2000 in Great Britain by
SUSSEX ACADEMIC PRESS
Box 2950
Brighton BN2 5SP

and in the United States of America by
SUSSEX ACADEMIC PRESS
5804 N.E. Hassalo St.
Portland, Oregon 97213-3644

British Library Cataloguing in Publication Data
A CIP catalogue record for this book is available from the British Library.

Library of Congress Cataloging-in-Publication Data
Shoham, Snunith.
Library classification and browsing: the conjunction of readers and documents /
Snunith Shoham.
p.   cm.
Includes bibliographical references and index.
ISBN 1–902210–55–7 (acid-free paper)
1. Library browsing.   2. Libraries and readers.   3. Open and closed shelves.   4.
Classification—Books.   I. Title.
Z711 .S36   2000
025.8'1—dc21   00–032222

Printed by Biddles Ltd, Guildford and King's Lynn
This book is printed on acid-free paper

Contents

List of Tables   vii
Preface   viii

**1   Technology and Concepts of Knowledge
     Organization**   1
     Technology and Society   2
     Technology and the Library   7

2   Shelf Arrangement: Storage   15

3   Shelf Arrangement: Intellectual Classification   33

4   Access to the Shelves   57

5   The Accessibility of Materials   75
     Factors Connected to Physical Aspects of the Library
        and the Organization of its Materials   76
     Factors Connected to Library Policy   80
     Factors Connected to the Method of Stock Management   81
     Factors Connected to the Intellectual System of Organizing
        the Materials   83

6   Concepts of Browsing   91

7   Browsing as an Information Retrieval Tool   103
     Effectiveness of Browsing   116

8 The Conjunction of Readers and Documents   **123**
Documentation   123
Accessibility   124
Channels of Mediation   125
Encounters without Mediatory Tools   133

Bibliography   139
Index   159

List of Tables

1.1   The technology of documents   11
1.2   Technology of catalogs   12
7.1   Sources of information on reading room materials   114
7.2   Means of discovery and usefulness of books   118

Preface

This book is the first in a series which will deal with theoretical concepts of organization of the library, of knowledge, and of information technology. The focus is on shelf arrangement of library materials from the physical and intellectual standpoints, and on the approach to library materials in terms of direct access that enables browsing, along with other factors that affect ease of access.

The book surveys intellectual concepts of arrangement of library materials, from the libraries of antiquity to those of the 1990s. These elements are discussed with regard to the physical format of the documents as well as the internal architectural design of the library, which on the one hand is a product of its time and on the other is necessarily adapted to the physical format of the documents. The different approaches to library materials over time will be examined, as well as issues of access and retrieval.

Chapter 1 details the close link between technology and the theoretical concepts of library classification. **Chapter 2** focuses on the physical aspect of shelf arrangement as it is influenced by technology. Here the relevant technologies are the publication format and the architect knowledge of the time, which affect the mode of storage of documents containing the wealth of knowledge of the period.

Chapter 3 considers the intellectual concepts according to which the documents are placed within the library. **Chapter 4** discusses the public's direct access to library collections. **Chapter 5** surveys the factors that affect ease of access to library materials.

Chapters 6 and 7 discuss browsing, which constitutes direct access via a channel of information search. **Chapter 8**, the concluding chapter, deals with the conjunction of readers with documents.

The book was written during the author's sabbatical in the summer of 1997 at the University of Alberta, Edmonton. The Canadian serenity was conducive to writing, and the personnel at the Department of Library and Information Studies at the university were most helpful and I would like to express my deep gratitude to them.

The research which formed the basis for this book was sponsored by the Cahann Ever Fund, the Ministry of Education and Culture of the State of Israel.

I

Technology and Concepts of Knowledge Organization

Technology encompasses the "vast universe of objects used by mankind to cope with the physical world, to delight our fancy, and to create symbols of meaning" (Schlereth, 1982, p. 2). What motivates technological invention? Some people believe that technology exists primarily to supply humanity with its most basic needs. Others maintain that technology's main purpose is to achieve well-being and the good-life. These notions change from one period to another, and what is considered a necessity at one place and time may not be regarded thus elsewhere (Basalla, 1988). Some scholars have sought to explain the development of technologies in terms of Darwin's theory of evolution (e.g. Pitt-Rivers, 1906; Butler, 1968).

Technological progress cannot be separated from the political and economic forces operating within a given society. Commercial self-interest is a major stimulus in the development and marketing of technological, consumer-oriented innovations (Musmann, 1993). Karl Marx was one of the first to offer an economic explanation for technological changes, when he noted that the development of the cotton gin by Eli Whitney was a response to a growing demand for cheap cotton and the limited availability of slaves to process the raw material manually.

But not every technological innovation is quickly adopted by society. Sometimes it is not clear at first what purpose a technological development will serve. Feenberg (1995) asserts that social meaning and functional rationality are intertwined dimensions of technology. Technological developments open pathways, but the final determination of the "right" pathway is made by society; hence, we can only understand technological development by studying the sociopolitical situation of the relevant group under discussion.

The Minitel system of computers, for example, the French government introduced as a device for centralized distribution of information; the purpose was to give telephone subscribers access to databases. However, the system's users used it mainly for human communication, specifically for anonymous on-line chatting with other users in search of amusement, companionship, and sex.

The directing of funds to space research or military buildup can lead to development of particular areas of technology. This can foster the development of further, accessory technologies or even complete industries. Often, technological innovations developed for a certain purpose turn out to be relevant to other areas of life. Thus, the nuclear power reactor was a direct outgrowth of the military uses of nuclear energy. The development of the atomic bomb by the United States during World War II led to the growth of the nuclear power industry.

Technologies, however, do not develop in a vacuum but are produced to satisfy real social requirements. The development of mechanical clocks in medieval monasteries was related to the importance monks attached to regular prayer observance; Henry Ford's decision to mass-produce an inexpensive car, as well as Apple's decision to market a personal home computer, reflect American values of individual freedom and convenience (Vig, 1998).

Technology and Society

At the same time, once a technology is discovered, produced, or developed it influences society; the conduct of life; different social institutions, including libraries; culture; and attitudes and beliefs.

Since technologies determine the conduct of life to a large extent, they are seen as demarcating historical periods.

In the Middle Ages, new power sources such as the watermill, along with windmill technology, constituted a use of non-human power. Therefore, instead of using slave labor, people developed a reliance on natural power sources. The implication was quite drastic, bringing the dependence on slave labor to an end (Basalla, 1988).

Several centuries later, the development of the ability to utilize created energy instead of relying on natural energy, brought the new era of industrial society. The invention of the steam engine by John Watt in 1775 was a major breakthrough, followed by the development of other created energies such as coal, gas, electricity, and nuclear power.

These energies made possible the use of machines with manufactory capacity, and opened the way to a new era in which the central economic activity was the manufacture and distribution of goods, and the main economic bodies were manufacturing and distributive industries. These replaced the extractive industries of preindustrial society in which people engaged in forestry, fishing, agriculture and mining.

The technological development that brought the establishment of the manufacturing industries transformed the social order and caused changes in the ways people lived. To begin with, cities grew and people began to migrate from villages to the cities to work in industry. This brought, in turn, changes in social power distribution: in the institution of the family, from the extended family to the nuclear family; and a rise in both the age of marriage, and births out of wedlock. Indeed, the institution of the family underwent a drastic transition from a unit of economic production to a unit based on the ties between its members.

The eighteenth century saw changes in the work environment as the growth of large industries brought a change in work methods. This constituted a transition from the former system, in which artisans and home industries completed the process of manufacturing from beginning to end, to a new system of the division of labor (Borgman, 1984).

In the late nineteenth century, a distinction developed

between ownership and management. This occurred first in Germany at the *Deutsche Bank*; a little later J. P. Morgan, Andrew Carnegie, and John D. Rockefeller used this approach in their massive restructuring of American railroads and industries (Drucker, 1988).

This change in the work environment brought by the industrial revolution also led to the emergence, in the late nineteenth and early twentieth centuries, of theories of organization that dealt with the integration of production within factories and the growth of large enterprises. These enterprises had new problems and needs that required innovative solutions.

The new industries were characterized by a concentration of raw materials, machines, and human beings in one place. This situation necessitated planning, coordination, central supervision, and more complex decision making. Different organizational structures emerged, among them the bureaucracy which, according to Max Weber, constituted a response to problems posed by large organizations. Weber maintained that feudalism, which suited agricultural society, had been replaced by a different social structure (Weber, 1964).

According to Weber, the characteristics of bureaucracy are: division of labor; centralization of authority: a firmly ordered system of super- and subordination in which there is a supervision of the lower offices by the higher offices; regular procedures; written documentation of all activities; and rational recruitment of employees.

The growth of a bureaucratic organizational structure came in the wake of the industrial revolution. In the late 1830s the largest American bank, Bank of United States, with 22 branches, was managed by only three people. In 1831, in the federal government under the administration of Andrew Jackson, there was a total of 665 civil servants. Fifty years later in the 1880s, in the wake of rapid industrialization, the Washington federal bureaucracy included 13,600 employees (Beniger, 1986).

Other scholars, among them Lilian and Frank Gilberth, Frederick Taylor, Henry Gratt and Harrington Emerson, who developed the School of Scientific Management in the early twentieth century, also developed time and motion studies, and emphasized, among other things, the clear distinction between manager and worker. A manager gifted with intelligence and planning ability, was responsible for planning the employees' work in all its details, while the employees were solely responsible for performing the work. The managers assumed the burden of amassing all of the traditional knowledge that in the past was possessed by the workers, and then classifying, tabulating, and reducing this knowledge to rules, laws, and formulas to direct the workers.

Modern management has replaced the traditional collegiality of the guilds with new forms of technical control, among them modern accounting techniques (1850s and 1860s), professional managers (1860s and 1870s), continuous-process production (late 1870s and early 1880s), Henry Ford's modern assembly line (after 1913), and statistical quality control (1920s). Among the first to introduce this new command-and-control organization were Pierre S. du Pont, when restructuring his family company, and Alfred P. Sloan, who redesigned General Motors (Drucker, 1988).

In the nineteenth century, far-reaching technological developments also occurred in the areas of transportation and communication. The first steam-powered railroad began operation in September 1830, and during the 1840s, 2,800 miles of railroad were laid in Britain. Attempts to produce road vehicles began late in the nineteenth century. Inventors in England, France and the United States separately devised the steam car, the electric car, and the gasoline car; eventually, the car powered by gasoline became the most popular method of transportation. The development of these means of transport made it easier for people to travel from the villages to the large cities and allowed them greater exposure to the world.

Communication technologies, including the telegraph and the telephone in the nineteenth century and the radio, the television, the fax, and telecommunication networks in the twentieth century enabled the transmission of information to all sectors of society in a short time, and with the most up-to-date technologies, even in real time. These inventions have facilitated the transition from the traditional rural village to the virtual, global village, and have contributed to the rise of the modern conception of democracy. Bell (1973) suggests that the development of computer and data transmission systems in the latter half of the twentieth century ushered in a new social era that he calls "postindustrial society," and which other scholars and intellectuals refer to as the "information society."

The technological developments of the twentieth century, particularly the computer and the whole array of devices based on computer technology, brought another radical change in the work environment. A hundred years after the rise of the hier-archical-bureaucratic organizational structure, this structure receded (Toffler, 1971) and more condensed, level organizational structures emerged in which the distinction between components of the organization was blurred. These encompass parallel organizations, matrix organizations, teams of experts, and even virtual work environments. The changes in human social life have also been expressed by changes in the human concept of time. With the industrial revolution, time was no longer measured by the seasons of the year, which were so important to agriculture, fishing, and hunting, dependent on seasonal weather changes, but rather by hours and fractions of hours.

More than a century ago, the introduction of artificial electrical lighting enabled human commercial and manufacturing activity without reference to daylight. Today's changing concept of time can be demonstrated by the new line of wrist-watches recently marketed by the Swatch Company. These watches measure time not in minutes or seconds (a concept based on the earth's daily revolving), but in "beats" of Internet virtual time. A 24-hour day is divided into 1,000 beats, each beat the equivalent of 1 minute, 26.4 seconds, so that in this system 12:00 noon (Central European Time) is @500 Swatch beats. The center of this new system is Biel, Switzerland, which is the location of the Swatch corporate head-quarters.[1] At the beginning of the third millennium, this new Internet time basically abrogates the need for time zones and by doing so indicates the lessening importance of the division of a day, especially in light of global research and business activities. Our changing perception of time reflects basic changes in our society.

[1] (http://www.swatch.com/internettime/internettime.php3)

Technology and the Library

Technologies have influenced not only political and social culture but also the role of the book and the library in society. One of mankind's more important early accomplishments was the invention of writing. The oldest writing was monumental and was inscribed on flat-sided stone pillars, on cylinders of stone or brick (in ancient Babylon), or on stone slabs (as were the hieroglyphic inscriptions of ancient Egypt); on clay tablets, which were later baked to give them durability (as were the tablets at Assurbani-pal's library in Assyria); on metal plates of copper or lead (in Greece, the works of Hesiod were inscribed on lead plates and deposited in the Temple of the Muses in Boeotia); and on wooden planks (the Laws of Solon were so recorded in Athens, where such tablets were used for public notices from the late fifth century BC). As the need in Greece for writing grew with the increase in education, animal skins were used (they had long been in use as a writing material in the Orient), or wax tablets, usually spread on a hard surface (commonly wood). The invention of writing thus required the creation of accompanying physical implements: the surface on which to write, and the writing tools themselves.

For centuries, the production of documents was cumbersome and expensive, and the technology was possessed by a select few. The invention of print in Europe by Johannes Gutenberg in the fifteenth century made the large-scale production of books an easier endeavor compared with the technologies that existed till then, which required the copying of each separate book by hand. The new and cheap technology enabled the distribution of books to wider audiences. This technological advance deeply influenced European society and led, among other things, to the Protestant revolt against the authority of the Roman Catholic Church, the rise of modern science, the growth of literacy and the spread of education.

The rise in the sophistication of Western societies is a product of technologies: the technology of printing, but also of manufacturing and mass-production, transportation and distribution, communication and data processing. As for libraries, the technologies that developed over the years influenced the arrangement of documents, the possibility of access to library materials, work methods within the library, the intellectual tools that developed to facilitate location of documents, and of course, the ways in which library clients were exposed to and made use of collections.

Developments in the architectural design of buildings influenced the arrangement of library materials, as well as library services. Here, one of the main factors was lighting. Up until the nineteenth century, libraries were dependent on natural light, hence, libraries were open only during daylight hours. The architectural planning of most library buildings reflected the reliance on natural light. In ancient times, library buildings (as well as temples) almost always faced the east. This gave access to the morning sun and ensured the dissipation of any night-time dampness, which was harmful to papyrus and parchment (Thompson, [1940] 1962). The proper installation of windows and the placement of shelves in relation to windows and skylights were of paramount importance to libraries (Musmann, 1993). High windows were recommended for reading rooms to maximize indoor brightness. On the other hand, in storage rooms the aim was to prevent the entrance of light so as to avoid harm to books.

From the middle of the nineteenth century, the use of gas lamps spread; toward the end of the nineteenth century the invention of electric light by Edison afforded another option for artificial lighting. The use of artificial illumination enabled libraries to stay open longer, though in the early years only the public areas were artificially lit. This technological change not only affected libraries' hours of operation; it also enabled additional groups of people to use library services, especially working men and women who could go to the library in the evenings after the day's work. This situation had far-reaching cultural and social effects.

The services that libraries provided also benefited from technology. Already by the late nineteenth century, certain reference services were provided by mail, such as bibliographies prepared in response to requests by correspondence. The provision of services by mail was of major significance, as this technology launched the ever-widening process of supplying library services to those not physically present in the library.

Other technologies facilitated this process, among them the telephone. The telephone was initially installed in the Library of Congress in 1901 and provided a connection between the main reading room and the Capitol building, enabling the ordering and receipt of books within a few minutes. Since the 1930s the telephone has been widely used in libraries, its main advantage being the provision of reference services to people outside the library, with libraries able to respond by telephone to all reasonable requests. Up to the present time, the telephone has mainly provided a ready-reference for factual information.

The development of such means of communication as teletype enabled a wide provision of inter-library loan services. The teletype machine was first introduced by the Free Library of Philadelphia, which in 1927 used it as part of a closed-circuit system for communicating book information from the loan desk in the main reading rooms to the stacks, and vice versa (Becker, 1969). Only in the 1970s was a new technology introduced into services for the public, one that has radically altered the way this service is provided, namely, the computer. The OCLC (Online Computer Library Center, a network for the provision of centralized services to libraries) pioneered the use of a computer in the inter-library loan service. It made possible the provision of up-to-the-minute information on thousands of other libraries and the placing of orders between libraries.

Other technologies have brought faster delivery of documents themselves. The fax machine enables immediate transmission of short documents. The CD ROM also serves as a technology for transmitting documents. An important pioneering venture is the Adonis project. In 1991 this project began to provide document delivery services – specifically, articles in the field of biomedicine, which were scanned together with keywords onto compact disks. From these it was possible to quickly extract any desired article, print it, and send it from the nearest service point. Service points were dispersed in a number of regions in the world. Recently a document delivery system called ARIEL has been offered to Internet users. It includes software and hardware together that enable the transfer of documents from place to place, from library to library, wherever in the world there is an ARIEL work station, and this by means of FTP (Internet file transfer protocol) or e-mail (MINE – multipurpose Internet mail extensions). ARIEL opens the door to desktop delivery: the library or information center will be able to deliver the online document directly to the end user's desktop.

One of the technologies that influenced library use, especially the use of non-fiction and reference collections, was the photo-copy machine. The first attempts to photocopy library material were made in the late nineteenth century. By the turn of the century, the Bibliothèque Nationale, the British Museum and most other European libraries had set up photographic dark-rooms in their institutions (Musmann, 1993). The development of photocopy machines began early in the twentieth century; the machines were then called "photostats." The Library of Congress and the New York Public Library were among the first to acquire and use a photostat, in 1912 (Malinconico, 1997).

In the 1950s, the Xerox Corporation first introduced its 914-copier. Unlike predecessors, this machine was simple enough for users to operate by themselves and made multiple copies in seconds. The introduction of photocopy machines to libraries, and their availability to the public, altered patterns of library use. This technology enabled the production of a personal copy of part of a document (and sometimes of the entire document) and its removal from the library. Thus, personal possession of library material was made possible. This phenomenon led to a reduced need for sitting in library reading rooms, as clients could now read material outside of the library instead.

The basic relevant technology is the format of the document. We witness, over the course of history, a passage from clay tablets and papyrus, to parchment and paper, up to the digital format (see table 1.1).

Table 1.1 The technology of documents

Period	Technology
Ancient World	Tablets
	Papyrus scrolls
Middle Ages	Codex (parchments)
	Codex (paper)
Modern Period	Codex (printed)
21st Century	Digital

So long as documents were of clay or papyrus, which are relatively difficult and expensive to produce, their placement, presentation, and also the access to them were dictated by their physical form, vulnerability, and of course the architectural capability of the time. With the transition to parchment technologies and the codex format, and later to paper, modes of treatment, storage, and access to documents changed. The printing technology of the fifteenth century, and the computer technology that developed in the twentieth century, radically changed the organization of library material (a subject discussed in depth in **chapters 2–4**).

In older times, the intellectual search tools were made in the same way as the documents themselves – from engraving on clay boards (sometimes also on the wall of the library), to inscription on papyrus, to writing on paper, to the printing in the print house of library catalogs. Only in the late nineteenth century (if we ignore a few isolated anecdotes), with the beginning of the use of card catalogs, did a separation occur between the format of the catalog and the format of the documents. Technological innovations of the late nineteenth century were what enabled the transition to the card catalog. Malinconico asserts that for libraries the invention of means of setting type from hot metal was the most important technological innovation of the nineteenth century for libraries.

The invention of the linotype machine by Ottmar Mergenthaler, in 1886, led the Library of Congress to adopt this new technology for producing its catalog cards (Malinconico, 1997). In 1901, the Library of Congress began its card distribution service. This single application of technology led to the standardization of the catalog format and to uniform rules of cataloging for all US libraries. The fact that many libraries abandoned the original preparation of their own catalogs, and instead acquired the ready-made card catalogs produced by the Library of Congress, meant that all of these libraries had card catalogs of identical size, and indeed the catalogs of thousands of libraries were identical. All decisions about cataloging are made at one central venue, and all libraries essentially use an intellectual tool that is built on the same principles.

Malinconico (1977) even asserts that the Anglo-American code has been created as an indirect result of the application of this technology. For years, the catalog registered the details of documents on catalog cards by means of manual inscription, and later by means of the typewriter. The typewriter was indeed developed late in the nineteenth century, but it came into use in libraries only in the 1930s. By the 1950s, the typewriter was regarded as the library's most essential machine. In the 1960s, a new physical format for catalogs appeared, namely, microforms. Within a decade these were replaced by the computer format of automated catalogs, which have gradually evolved since 1966, with the first pilot project of MARC (Machine Readable Cataloging, developed by the Library of Congress), and especially since the 1980s, into the widely used format of electronic cataloging systems (see table 1.2). During this whole period, the main format for documentation was printing on paper.

Table 1.2 Technology of catalogs

Period	*Technology*
Ancient	The walls of world librarys
	Tablets
	Papyrus scrolls
Middle Ages	Codex (handwritten, paper)
15th Century	Codex (printed)
Late 19th Century	Handwritten cards
1930s	Typed cards
1960s	Microforms
1980s	Electronic records

The end of the twentieth century witnessed a gradual transition, which can be expected to continue in the next century, from documents to electronic format. In other words, after a hundred years there is again a similarity between the physical structure of the document and of the intellectual information system. The assumption that a link exists between, on the one hand, the technology of the book, and concepts about its arrangement and the possibilities of seeking the information contained in it, constitutes the basis for the subsequent chapters, which discuss the arrangement of books, their accessibility, and modes of locating them.
.

2

Shelf Arrangement: Storage

Libraries and archives already existed in very early periods of human history. Early libraries were located in rooms adjacent to a palace or a temple. The oldest library discovered is one that was excavated in the city of Ebla, in Syria, which served as an important trade center between the civilizations of Egypt and Mesopotamia, dating from around 2500–2200 BC. The library consists of over 14,000 clay tablets, representing the administrative records of a dynasty founded by King Igrish Kalam. The tablets include commercial treaties, bilingual vocabularies in Sumerian and Eblaite, lists of birds, fish and stone, many ritual and theological texts, diplomatic letters, military dispatches, and lists of personal and place names (Bermant and Weitzman, 1979; Nissen, 1988).

Another ancient library was in Nippur (circa 2000 BC); in one of its rooms (which was about 33 feet long and 17 feet wide), tablets were placed around the walls on wooden shelves.

In the palace of King Assur-bani-pal (668–631 BC), at Nineveh, archeological excavations discovered two chambers. One was 27 feet long, the second 23 feet; they were accessible from the entrance to the palace, and appeared to contain the decrees of the Assyrian kings, as well as archives of the empire (Clark, 1902). This library was one of the largest in the ancient world, believed to contain 25,000 to 30,000 tablets (Harris, 1995).

In Egypt, the best-known palace library was that at Tell-el-Amarna, a capital built by Amenhotep IV about 1350 BC. Here the remains of a library have been found in a room designated the "Place of the Records of the Palace of the King" (Harris, 1995).

In the ancient world, three forms of writing surface were used. One was the clay tablet, which was used from Persia to the Mediterranean from the fourth millennium BC into several centuries of the Christian era (Harris, 1995). The usual clay tablet was about 2–3 inches long and about an inch thick. Tablets were kept on narrow shelves, in shallow bins, sometimes in a pigeon-hole arrangement, sometimes in baskets or clay jars (Harris, 1995). In some late Babylonian libraries the clay tablets were displayed on shelves, but they were more commonly kept in clay boxes or earthen jars; the jars, in turn, were kept in orderly rows on shelves. Twig records were tied together in bundles, and the stringing together of records was one of the earliest and most extensively used methods of recording a collection (Richardson, 1963).

A second writing surface was the papyrus, which came from the trees that grew along the Nile and throughout the Mediterranean area. Papyrus was made from the pith of the stems, gummed strips of which were laid in two transverse layers and then crushed and rolled into thin wafers (Thompson, [1940] 1962). Thompson believes the use of papyrus was not confined to antiquity but continued until the eleventh century, mainly for diploma and material records. A complete strip of papyrus could form a roll from 10 to 30 feet long and from 6 to 10 inches wide. Practically, there was no limit to the length of a roll. Some ancient Egyptian papyri are more than 150 feet long, and in Greece the complete works of such authors as Homer and Herodotus were at first written on a single roll. But, since such huge rolls were inconvenient to hold, scholars adopted the practice of cutting up long rolls into shorter lengths. This led to the division of a literary work into several books (Thompson, [1940] 1962).

Small collections of rolls might be kept in pottery jars, but larger numbers were usually kept in niches or pigeonholes in the library walls (Harris, 1995). When a number of rolls had to be carried from one place to another, they were put into boxes (*scrinium* or *capsa*). These were cylindrical in shape and carried by a flexible handle attached to a ring on each edge (Clark, 1902).

Later, the use of the parchment roll began. In antiquity, the skin of sacrificial animals such as sheep and goats was used by the priests of all the religions for the writing of prayers, rituals, and liturgical matter (Thompson, [1940] 1962). The parchment roll, or vellum, came into general use in the second century. If the roll was special or precious, a jacket of parchment was provided (Clark, 1902).

The papyrus and the parchment rolls remained the dominant forms of written material throughout the Greek and Roman eras and continued to be used in Europe into the modern era. In the third century, pagan works were still generally written on rolls; the codex was the popular form for Christian books. The introduction of parchment popularized the codex form, since the parchment leaves could not be bound end-to-end like sheets of papyrus except by sewing them together. Accordingly, parchment sheets were put together like the pages of a modern book and the whole was bound between board covers (Thompson, [1940] 1962). By the fourth century AD, the codex was becoming widely used.

When codices had to be accommodated as well as rolls, the rectangular spaces, not more than a few inches wide, were no longer convenient. They were therefore discarded in favor of a press (*armarium*), a piece of furniture that held rolls as well as codices (Clark, 1902).

The libraries of classical Greece, which date from the sixth century BC to the third century AD, left few physical remains. Most of what is known about these libraries is derived from references to them in Greek and Roman literature. We can infer from our knowledge of the Alexandrian library in Egypt what were the characteristics of the Greek libraries. The Alexandrian library was erected by the Greek scholar Demetrius, who was familiar with the school of Aristotle; it was built for Ptolemy, who ruled Egypt early in the third century BC.

The Pergamon library was built by Eumenes II, who ruled for almost 40 years (197–159 BC) and was an energetic book collector. He constructed a city acropolis, a temple of Athena, and a library. Four rooms are believed to have been designated for library purposes. Two of them were 39 by 33 feet; the others were 39 by

23, and 42 by 49 feet, respectively (Clark, 1902). The library rooms were located off the northern colonnade of the temple. The largest room had a narrow platform about three feet high around three of its sides. Behind the platform, the walls had holes that may have held shelf brackets, or served to anchor bookcases (Harris, 1995).

Roman conquerors would bring books home as spoils of war. The first to do so was the general Paulus Aemilius in 168 BC (Harris, 1995). By 50 BC, private libraries were becoming common among the wealthy families of Rome; the only public collections were the temple and government archives.

Augustus was the first emperor to erect public buildings in Rome. In 33 BC he built two libraries on the Campus Martius, one for Greek books and the other for Latin books. A library of Apollo was built on the Palatine Hill (36–29 BC), again in two parts – one for Greek books and the other for Latin books. Between them was a hall, perhaps used as a reading room (Clark, 1902). All in all, 26 public libraries were built in Rome, in addition to private libraries in wealthy, private Roman homes. The greatest of the Roman libraries was the Ulpian, built by the emperor Trajan in 114 AD in his Forum. It was essentially a scholars' library and was situated behind the great basilica or the law courts (Thompson, [1940] 1962). Like other Roman libraries, it was divided into Greek and Latin sections.

Roman libraries included rooms for the storage of books and rooms for reading, although the colonnades, to which the libraries were usually adjacent, lent themselves to reading, or discussing books while walking (Harris, 1995). These reading rooms were frequently used for conversation, meditation, rhetorical contests, lectures, and public meetings (Thompson, [1940] 1962).

The books were at that time placed on a type of shelf called *pegmata*. These were usually planks of wood formed into a platform, and were used in theaters to carry pieces of scenery or performers up and down. As applied to books, their name probably meant "shelves." Clark (1902) suggests that so long as only rolls had to be accommodated, private libraries in Rome were fitted with rows of shelves standing against the walls (*pluei*), or affixed to them (*pegmata*). The spaces between these horizontal shelves were subdivided by vertical divisions into pigeonholes (*nidi, foruli, loculamenta*). The width of these pigeonholes would vary in accordance with the number of rolls included in a single work (Clark, 1902).

The organization and handling of the rolls in the Roman libraries were similar to that in the Greek libraries; however, the Romans added the *armarium* (press) for keeping more valuable rolls (Harris, 1995). The Ulpian libraries in Trajan's Forum were filled with presses; up to the late seventh century, this was the usual storage method (Clark, 1902). In excavations in Herculaneum, a popular resort located between Naples and Pompeii, rolls that were remnants of a small private library were found. Some 1,700 rolls were discovered placed in wooden presses (*armaria*), of a man's height, that stood around the room against the walls (Clark, 1894). In the middle of the room there was another, similar bookcase, or table for writing (Clark, 1902).

In the sixth century, Cassiodorus, a Roman noble who for many years served the Ostrogoth kings as their Latin secretary, established on one of his estates a monastery called Vivarium. He built there a library to which he donated his private books, and then started to collect manuscripts. Cassiodorus introduced the practices of copying manuscripts and of translating valuable Greek works into Latin (Thompson, 1939). At about the same time Saint Benedict, who established the Benedictine Order and founded several monasteries in Italy and Western Europe, promulgated the "Rules" for the daily life of a monastery. Under these rules, the reading and copying of books were part of the regular monastic routine (Johnson, 1970). Thus, during the Middle Ages the monasteries became the centers for the maintenance and reading of books.

The center of monastic life was the cloister. There the books were kept, and the monks wrote and studied, or conducted the schooling of the novice. Often the press was located in a niche in the wall, a practice that began in Roman times. In the wall of the cloister, recesses were usually located near the Chapter House or just inside the entrance to it. Later came *armaria* for books, fitted with wooden shelves and doors. Sometimes the *armarium*, instead of being a cupboard in the wall, was a piece of standing furniture fitted with shelves and doors (Streeter, 1931). A rare description of a press (*armarium*) appeared in the "Customs" of the Augustinian Order at Barnwell, England:

> The press in which the books are kept ought to be lined inside with wood, that the damp of the walls may not moisten or stain the books. This press should be divided vertically as well as horizontally by sundry shelves on which the books may be ranged so as to be separated from one another; for fear they be packed so close as to injure each other or delay those who want them.
>
> (Clark, 1902, p. 61)

As of the thirteenth century, codices in Europe were made of paper, although paper was used even earlier in southern Italy (Thompson, 1939). Paper also contributed to the increase in publications.

So long as quantities of books were small these presses sufficed. But as the monastery collection grew and exceeded 250–350 books, new presses had to be placed in the cloister. Later, with still more books added to the collection, more chambers were built in which books were kept on sets of shelves (*collumpnoe*) set against the wall. These rooms were small and used only for storage purposes, and were usually near the cloister (Streeter, 1931).

Use of additional rooms began in the twelfth century. Reading and copying were done in the cloister. At some point in the thirteenth century a system of tiny studies (carrels) was developed, each of which was provided with a desk and a stool to accommodate a single work. These carrels were set against the windows of the cloister. At Durham, a row of three carrels for each window was the arrangement (Streeter, 1931).

About the beginning of the fourteenth century, four different ways of dealing with books emerged: the lectern or desk, to which one or more books were chained; the *armaria* and chest, in which books were locked up; the carrels, in which books could be read; and in some monasteries a room or rooms that were used for storage only (Streeter, 1931).

At Durham, the catalog made in 1395 enumerated:

(1) "the books in the common press at Durham in sundry places in the cloister" (386 volumes);
(2) "the books in the common press at Durham in the Spendment" (408 volumes);
(3) "the inner library at Durham called Spendment" (87 volumes);
(4) "the books for reading in the frater which lie in the press near the entrance to the farmery" (17 volumes);
(5) "the books in the common press of the novices at Durham in the cloister" (23 volumes).

(Clark, 1902, p. 97)

At Citeaux, a large wealthy monastery in Burgundy, the books were dispersed. We learn about this from the catalog compiled by Abbot John de Cirey in the late fifteenth century, which mentions 1,200 manuscripts and a few printed books. In a room at the top of a staircase were six bookcases, called benches, as well as cupboards (*armaria*). This room held a total of 509 books. In addition, the catalog enumerates: books of the choir, church, and cloister (53 volumes); books taken out of the library for the daily use of the convent (29 volumes); books chained on desks before the Chapter House (5 volumes); books on the second desk (5 volumes); books on the third desk (4 volumes); books on the fifth desk (4 volumes); books taken out of the library partly to be placed in the cloister, partly to be divided among the brethren (27 volumes); books on the small desks in the cloister (5 volumes); books to be read publicly in the convent or to be divided among the brethren for private reading (99 volumes) (Clark, 1902, pp. 99–100). There were a total of 740 books scattered around the monastery.

This multitude of books dispersed among the various rooms of the monasteries brought many monasteries to the decision to establish a real library. For example, at Christ Church, Canterbury, a library about 60 feet long by 22 feet wide was built by Archbishop Chichele between 1414 and 1443. A library was established in Durham by Prior Wessyngton in 1446, and in many other monasteries special rooms were built or designed for this purpose.

In the thirteenth century and later, more books were stored in these libraries on lecterns of wood – that is, laid flat on their sides on a slanted desk surface that was both storage and reading space; often these books were chained (Boll, 1985). The height of the desk was convenient for a seated reader to use. A bench for the reader was placed between each pair of desks (Clark, 1902). The lectern had a desk on each side; the books were chained to a rod just above the peak of the desk. Clark (1902) called this system of shelving and reading the *lectern system.*

The emergence of universities brought with it the development of academic libraries. A "real library" – that is, a room expressly designed for the purpose of containing books – was not introduced into the plan of universities for more than a century after their emergence. Such rooms could at once be recognized by their equidistant windows, which were separated by much smaller intervals than in the ordinary chambers.

One of the earliest of these libraries was built by Thomas Cobham (bishop of Worcester, 1317–27) on the north side of St. Mary's Church, Oxford, about 1320. The room was 45 feet long by 18 feet wide, and had seven single-light windows on each side, and a window of two lights at the east end.

The collections of the university libraries were usually divided in two, one part for lending and one for immediate use. The old College Statutes at Oxford and at Cambridge imply a division of the community books into two groups. The more valuable were kept chained in the library; others, especially textbooks and duplicates, were lent to the Fellows, usually at a solemn assembly held once a year (Streeter, 1931).

At Peterhouse, Cambridge, in 1418, out of a total of 302 books, 143 were said to be chained, and 125 were assigned for distribution among Fellows (the other 34 books were probably set aside to be sold) (Streeter, 1931). Sometimes the books available for lending, when not actually lent, were kept in chests in the treasury. The Statutes of Peterhouse, Cambridge (1344), prescribed that: "The aforesaid books, charters, and muniments are to be placed in one or more common chests, each having two locks, one key of which shall for greater security be deposited with the

Master, the other with the Senior Dean" (Clark, 1902, p. 128).

Practices in the university libraries were very similar to those in the monasteries. Many collegiate libraries were built at the same time as some of the monastic ones. The similarity between monastic and secular practices reflected the fact that some of the founders of the colleges were religious figures or had been educated in the monasteries, and thus had experience of monastic libraries. There was also a direct monastic influence on the universities through their student-monks. At Oxford, which was specially designated as the university for monastic colleges, the Benedictines founded Gloucester House as early as 1283.

In addition, the books for the libraries of some of these universities came initially from the parent monastery. Sometimes the library furniture came from the same source. Some universities did not maintain a real library at first, but only after some time. For example, at Merton College, Oxford, founded in 1264, the library was not established until 1377. At University College, founded in 1280, the library was created only in 1440. William of Wykeham, who founded the New College, Oxford, in 1380, was the first to include a library in his quadrangle.

Many university libraries were established at the same time as monastery libraries. In the fifteenth century, monasteries began to allot space and build separate libraries, and cathedrals also began to build libraries. The cathedral of Lincoln was a timber structure built between 1419 and 1426 above a stone cloister (Streeter, 1931). It is probable that in its library there was originally a row of windows in the east wall and another in the west wall, one to each bay on each side, the walls being divided by vertical shafts into bays, each 7 feet, 9 inches wide. Among other early cathedral libraries, the library at Salisbury was founded in 1444–5; the chapter library at Wells Cathedral (founded in 1424) was about 162 feet long by 12 feet wide; and the cathedral library at Troyes, built by Bishop Louis Raghier between 1477 and 1479, was nearly square, 30 feet long by 24 feet wide, and the books were contained in six desks. This library was called La Théologale because lectures on theology were given there (Clark, 1902).

In the fifteenth century, both monastery and college libraries often took the form of a long, narrow room lighted by rows of equidistant windows. An example is the Queens' College Library, Cambridge (1448), which was on the first floor. It was 44 feet long by 20 feet wide and was lighted by 11 windows, each with two lights. The distance between each pair of windows was no more than two feet. This was a common library structure in England, France, the Netherlands, Germany, and Italy at least into the seventeenth century.

The fittings consisted of lecterns of wood. On these the books were laid, each volume fastened by a chain to a bar usually placed over the desk, but occasionally in front or beneath it. The readers sat on benches immovably fixed opposite each window. Reading was convenient enough so long as the students were few, but if they were numerous and the books chained too closely together, much annoyance must have resulted (Clark, 1902). With the growth in the number of books, the lectern-system library became very crowded. The books stood next to each other on the shelf, and a person who was using one of them blocked others' access to the adjacent books. Therefore the two halves of the desk were separated, with a larger interval than before, or sometimes a broader lectern with one or more shelves fixed above it.

Libraries now began to feature bookcases, containing at least four shelves, two to each side of the case, which could be made as long as the width of the library permitted. Clark (1902) called this the *stall system*, "stall" being derived from the word *staulum* (or *stallum*), which was used in the Middle Ages for bookcases. The stall system combined a lectern with an *armarium*. To the lectern partitions, cupboard divisions were added (Streeter, 1931). This arrangement first appeared in Magdalen College, Oxford, in 1480. It was the practice at Corpus Christi College, Oxford, in 1517; in St. John's College, Oxford, in 1596; and in Sir Thomas Bodley's library, Oxford, in 1598. From Oxford colleges it spread to other institutions, and became the common system in England and France in the seventeenth century.

In the stall-system library, the books stood upright on a shelf rather than on their sides, so it was necessary to attach the chain in a different manner. The chains were now longer, according to the shelf on which the books stood, to enable moving them to the desk and reading them.

The library rooms were now larger; a typical library was 86 feet by 32 feet. By the seventeenth century, the stall library stored many rows of books. The stalls were typically arranged in alcove form with seating in between; the intervals between the large bookcases now afforded small study areas, or sometimes were arranged even more closely in a stack-like set-up. These arrangements became widespread by the late eighteenth century. Examples are the libraries of Edinburgh University, founded in 1825, and of Copenhagen University, founded in 1857 (Boll, 1985).

In the fifteenth century, libraries had become very prominent in Europe – in religious as well as secular institutions, in monasteries, cathedrals, and universities. In the sixteenth century, with the decline in monasteries brought about by the Huguenot movement in France and the suppression of the monastic orders in England, libraries, too, declined. By 1540, the only libraries in England were those of the two universities and in cathedrals of the Old Foundation. Many books were removed, sometimes sold. In 1549, commissioners were sent by Edward VI to Oxford and Cambridge to reconstitute the libraries.

The emergence of print led to a decrease in the price of books, and new libraries did not return to the old systems. The first library built and furnished under these new conditions was that of St. John's College, Cambridge (1623–8). Libraries still consisted of a long, narrow room (about 30 feet by 110 feet). However, books were no longer fastened by chains to a desk. Consequently it was no longer necessary to provide either a desk or a seat. Instead of the desk (which characterized the ancient and old libraries), a low bookcase was placed in front of each window. These cases were 5 feet, 6 inches high, with a sloping desk on the top, on which books could be laid for study.

Toward the end of the eighteenth century, the practice of chaining books was finally abandoned. In the Bodleian Library, Oxford, the removal of the chains began in 1757. At King's College, Cambridge, the books were unchained in 1777. In France, the practice was abandoned much earlier (Clark, 1902).

In Continental Europe, a new system of shelving evolved in which the bookshelves were set against the wall. The central parts of the hall were mostly empty, occasionally housing a few reading tables. This arrangement was first introduced into the library at the Escorial, started by Philip II of Spain in 1563 and completed in 1584. There were, probably, other libraries of this type by the late sixteenth century. The Escorial library was 212 feet long by 35 feet wide and about 36 feet high. It was lighted by five windows on the east side and seven on the west, as well as five smaller windows on the east side, under the vault. The principal windows were 13 feet high and extended down to the floor. The wall spaces between each pair of windows had bookcases fitted to them; these bookcases were more than 12 feet high. Desks were 2 feet, 7 inches high.

Between 1603 and 1609, Cardinal Federigo Borromeo built the Bibliotheca Ambrosiana at Milan. Here again, the bookcases were lined against the wall. Light entered through two enormous semi-circular windows at each end of the room, and in each corner of the room there was a staircase to the gallery. Similarly, the library of Cardinal Mazarin (Paris, 1647) had a large room, bookcases set against the walls, and a gallery.

The first library in England that adopted the new system was the Bodleian Library, Oxford, built in 1610–12. This enabled storage of books from the floor to the ceiling (the access to the high part being through the gallery; there, the books were still chained). The desks were still set against the bookshelves.

The architect Sir Christopher Wren contributed to the spread of the *wall system* in England. In 1674 he built a library at Lincoln Cathedral; in 1675–6, he built one for Trinity College in Cambridge. In the College Library the books were placed against the wall, sometimes facing the room. In the Jesuits' library in France (1678), the books were placed five feet from the wall; thus, quiet corners for study were created between the bookcases. The space between the shelves and the wall was used for storage. The Bibliothèque Sainte-Geneviève (Paris, 1675) was built in a similar style (and had two galleries), as was the library of Saint-Germain-des-Prés (Paris) (Clark, 1902).

The central parts of the library halls were mostly empty, sometimes decorated with large globes, but occasionally had a few reading tables. Around 1800 this was the common structure for libraries, especially on the European continent (Boll, 1985). Over the centuries the increasing numbers of books forced libraries to expand by building higher walls, then by building galleries, and by expanding into adjoining rooms (Boll, 1985).

As libraries grew larger, a new system of wall shelving was introduced. This in time led to a reduction in the size and number of windows, so that galleries could be installed for convenient access to the shelves as they mounted toward the high ceilings. Some libraries added alcoves along the walls. Reading tables were placed in the alcoves and also in the center of the library (Wheeler and Githens, [1959] 1978). In these hall-type libraries, books, readers, and librarians were intermingled. The chief infusion of light came from the great ceiling of the hall. Before the nineteenth century, most of the libraries in the United States as well as in Europe were of the hall type (Bishop, 1947).

The nineteenth century saw a further increase in book production; changes in higher education that required more space for books, readers, and library staff; and the establishment of the public library as literacy spread and readers were no longer a restricted clientele.

All these factors, together with the newly established professions of architecture and librarianship, caused a decline in the hall-type library. Instead, efforts were made to meet the new functional needs of libraries by "tripartitioning," i.e., allocating space for three separate functions: book storage, reader accommodations, and staff work areas (Kaser, 1986). Thus, from the mid-nineteenth century a division occurred among the three main components of the library: books, readers, and librarians.

The view now was that the service could not be performed by the readers themselves as in the past, but must instead be performed by librarians. There was one point of contact between the readers and the librarians, namely, the delivery desk, where readers borrowed and returned books. This delivery desk was placed midway between the public and the books. Winsor (1876, pp. 466–7) described a new branch of the Boston Public Library that had "a book room 27 feet wide by 55 feet long and 24 feet high; the desk of delivery being midway on one of the longer sides, just without a door which opens into a waiting apartment."

In the 1880s, the influential architect Henry Hobson Richardson designed library buildings that reflected the transition from the hall-type library to libraries with separate stack and reading rooms.

The Boston Public Library, designed by Charles Follen McKin, became a model for public libraries throughout the United States: book stacks in the rear, one great room across the front on the second floor. The Boston Public Library also influenced college and university libraries, which had enormous reading rooms on the main floor and closed book stacks at the rear.

In Europe, this basic design could be seen in the Bavarian Royal Library in Munich (1843), the Sainte-Geneviève Abbey's library in Paris (1843), and the British Museum in London (1856) (Boll, 1985). By the 1870s, the concept of separate reading rooms and separate stacks was commonly accepted in Europe, as in the large libraries in America.

The separation between the book room and the reading room enabled maximal utilization of the book storage rooms. As Winsor, director of the Boston Public Library, explained, the main idea of the modern public library building was compact storage to save space, and short distances to save time. The bottoms of the windows in the book room of the Boston Public Library were eight feet from the floor, giving an unbroken wall of shelving around the room. Then, two rows of ten double-face cases were placed standing crosswise. As for the reading room, Winsor (1876, p. 471) asserts that "a large room with stalls, or a series of apartments with tables and shelf convenience, should be provided for students making protracted investigations, and wishing to keep the books they use at their desks from day to day."

In the 1930s and 1940s, a new concept of library planning emerged. Precursors had appeared even earlier; for instance, the Springfield (Massachusetts) Public Library, designed in 1912 by Edward L. Tilton, was actually the first library to use the concept later known as the *open plan* (Baumann, 1972).

The open-plan libraries came hand-in-hand with the new concept of open shelves. In 1890, the Cleveland Public Library was the first to grant access to the shelves to the general public, and this was reflected in the design of its new building in 1925. The Enoch Pratt Free Library in Baltimore (1933), which was also an open-plan library, influenced later buildings. In these libraries book stacks relied on artificial lighting, and the books used were shelved in the reference room on the main floor, which was large and convenient with easy and attractive access (Wheeler and Githens, [1959] 1978). All in all, open-plan concepts spread slowly.

It was Angus Snead Macdonald, president (1916–25) of Snead & Co., which built library book stacks, who introduced open-space, flexible libraries in the United States. In the framework of his company, he designed a new kind of stack (the hollow-column feature) that could be more easily altered. He also developed compact shelving for less-used materials.

In the period after World War II, Macdonald's ideas began to attract attention. Many library buildings, particularly in the college and university domain, benefited from his concepts, and from the late 1940s there was a trend in favor of the modular plan.

The general use of modular buildings in new university libraries after World War II reflected, first, the changes in the universities. These institutions had grown drastically, and with them their libraries. Universities had also changed a great deal in research and teaching programs, and in teaching methods. Since the 1930s, enlightened educators (including librarians) had increasingly stressed the importance of library work (Ellsworth, 1973). It became clear that the buildings that would house the changing book collections and respond to the needs of changing programs would have to permit easy reorganization and expansion, while remaining as functional as the original buildings.

The modular design that was introduced into American library-building planning following World War II, and then spread to Denmark and Britain, was fully accepted by the 1960s.

The growth in the size of the library collections brought different strategies. These often included on-site or remote storage facilities, weeding, resource sharing, as well as new storage systems. The most common of the new storage systems were compact shelving, which is less convenient for users; automated storage, which is suitable only for closed stacks; and shelving by other criteria than book content, such as book size. The shortage of room for storage together with the development of technology brought about new book formats (such as microforms and electronic formats) that, again, required new storage strategies.

Summary

In ancient times, documents were recorded on clay tablets, papyrus rolls, and later on parchment. The methods of storage and arrangement were varied according to the format of the document. Tablets were kept in clay jars, in baskets on narrow shelves, or in pigeonholes. Papyrus and parchment rolls were kept in jars or in niches and pigeonholes in the library walls. When codices came into use, they were accommodated in presses. During the Middle Ages, books in monasteries were usually kept in the cloister in a press that was located in a niche of the wall. When more books were added to the collection, small chambers for storage purposes were built.

In the thirteenth century and later, books for reading were kept on a lectern that had desks on both sides; a stool for the reader was placed between each pair of desks. These desks were set against the windows. With the increase in the number of books, this lectern-system library became very crowded, and in the fifteenth century a stall system was developed. In this system the two halves of the desk were separated, and the lectern contained at least four shelves, two to each side. In both of these systems, books were chained, although in different manners.

Toward the end of the eighteenth century the practice of chaining books was finally abandoned, and a new system of shelving was developed: bookcases now faced the wall. Books were placed on shelves along the walls from the ceiling to the floor. In these wall-system libraries, readers and books were intermingled. However, during the nineteenth century, with a further increase in the numbers of books and of library users, a separation between books and readers emerged. New libraries contained separate reading areas and storage rooms, with the librarians placed in between. During the 1930s and 1940s, a new concept of library design appeared, namely, the modular library. Along with this change came the concept of free access to the shelves and the reintegration of readers with books.

The vast growth of libraries into large institutions, some with millions of books, that occurred in the 1950s and 1960s forced libraries to seek more economical storage systems. This resulted in storage at least of large parts of collections in warehouses closed to the public, in which economical storage systems were used with books arranged not according to subject but again according to the size of the books or by accession number.

3

Shelf Arrangement: Intellectual Classification

Classification of materials began very early. The distinction between temple and palace libraries in ancient times can be regarded as a materials classification, as was the distinction between shamans and secular recorders. Also, as early as 2700 BC in Egypt and quite early in Crete, like kinds of work, such as medical works, were placed in boxes together (Richardson, 1963).

In Mesopotamia, temple libraries contained histories of the gods; texts of formal rituals, hymns, incantations, invocations, prayers, sacred epics, and scriptures; as well as works on agriculture, biology, mathematics, astronomy, and medicine. Palace libraries contained the government's documents, such as laws and legal decisions, official letters, orders to military officials, commercial records, and tax lists; as well as biographies of officials, information on neighboring countries, and descriptions of towns and countries (Harris, 1995).

There is insufficient information on how the Babylonian and Sumerian libraries were organized. However, from the time of the Assyrians, remnants of true libraries, arranged by subject matter and available through a primitive form of catalog, were discovered. Excavation in southern Babylon (Sumer) of a temple library, which contained about 25,000 to 30,000 tablets, indicate that those tablets were probably placed on the shelves according to some sort of subject classification (Hyman, 1972).

The Assyrian King Sargon II (772–705 BC) developed a palace library at Korshabad. His grandson Assur-bani-pal (ca. 668–627 BC) moved the capital to Nineveh. In his palace, two chambers, accessible from the entrance to the library, were found to contain the decrees of the Assyrian kings as well as the archives of the empire. About 25,000 tablets were placed in these rooms. It is believed that these tablets were arranged on the shelves in systematic subject order. Already in antiquity, related works in large collections were kept together.

Catalogs in Mesopotamian libraries accorded with the shelf order. These catalogs, which have survived from antiquity, indicate that some rough subject order was already maintained for tablets and rolls in earthen jars (Rovelstad, 1976). However, the subject arrangement was not based on an abstract framework of universal knowledge but on literary warrant, and on the collection of which they were a part (Hyman, 1982). Some works were part of a series: for example, the epic of the creation (*Enuma elish*) occupied seven tablets and the *Gilgamesh* epic occupied 12 tablets (Weitemeyer, 1956). In Mesopotamian libraries, mathematical and astrological texts were also sometimes part of a series. Weitemeyer suggests that the motive for making these series must have been to amass all literature on the same subject in one place.

Thompson ([1940] 1962, p. 9) asserts that tablets in collections or libraries in the temples and palaces of Babylonia and Assyria were numbered in different series according to their placements in the library. Every series was named according to the words or sentence that headed the first tablet, and each succeeding tablet had its proper number, thus, "Sixteenth tablet of the evil spirits."

In ancient Egypt, the temple library began as a collection of sacred scriptures. Then, books of rituals were added. Gradually these libraries came to include also secular literature, since medicine and astronomy were closely connected with Egyptian religion (Harris, 1995). One of the oldest library catalogs was found in Egypt on the wall of the temple library of Edfu, known as the House of Papyrus (300–200 BC). The title on the wall says: "List of cases containing the books on great rolls of skins." The books were divided into two categories: 12 coffers of books are specified in the first list, and 22 in the second. According to Thompson ([1940] 1962), there is evidence of logical classification: the second list or catalog contained works on magic. The catalog of the Ptolemaic Temple of Hathor at Denberah (117 BC) appears to have a systematic order, which argues in favor of some system of classification (Sperry, 1957).

Although it is known that in ancient Greece there were public as well as private libraries, no remnants have been found. Aristotle is known to have had a collection of books and to have been the first to work out an arrangement of books by a definite system, believed to have been adopted afterward by the Ptolemies at Alexandria (Clark, 1902).

Demetrius of Phaleron, the Greek scholar who was invited by Ptolemy I to Alexandria, initiated the establishment of a "university," a museum (or "temple of the muses," where scholars could work), and a library. This library, established around 295 BC, became the largest of the ancient period; some believe it contained no less than 200,000 volumes by the end of Ptolemy's reign (Parsons, 1952).

Callimachus, the librarian of the Alexandrian library (260–240 BC), prepared the "*Pinakes*." The word *pinax* means "tablet" and may have been the name used for tablets placed over the library cases to indicate their contents (Witty, 1958). Later the word was used to refer to a list of authors. In the Alexandrian library, authors were arranged according to their type of literature, and such categories were perhaps kept in separate halls. Each division constituted at least one *pinax* (Parsons, 1952).

We cannot tell into how many divisions, classes or *Pinakes* the entire body of Greek literature was divided. We do know about some of the divisions: poets, lawmakers, philosophers, historians, rhetoricians (orators), miscellaneous writers (Richardson, 1963), and probably also writers on medicine (Parsons, 1952; Witty, 1958). Of the above categories only three – Laws, Oratory, and Miscellaneous – are *Pinakes* fragments; scholars have learned about the others from references to them in various works (Parsons, 1952).

We also have many indications of subdivisions, such as, under Poetry: epic, comic, tragic, dithyrambic; and also: Birds, Fishes,

Geometry, Medicine, Feasts, and so on (Richardson, 1963). For the orators, Callimachus seems to have divided the orations according to purpose: Official (state-political), Professional (matters of law), and civic. The arrangement of Demosthenes' speeches is generally attributed to Callimachus (Parsons, 1952). The subdivisions seem to have been, in some cases at least, chronological by period, and at least for the short miscellaneous subjects, probably alphabetical by author (Witty, 1958; Richardson, 1963).

Roman libraries closely followed the collection arrangements of the Greek and Hellenistic libraries. From the breakdown of the Roman Empire until the later Middle Ages, complex shelving techniques were not needed because collections were small. The monastery libraries had very small collections compared with those of antiquity. Since the books had to be used where they were, a rough subject order was the typical form of organization. For a long period, the arrangement itself had to serve as a finding device since there were no catalogs (Rovelstad, 1976).

The earliest medieval catalogs were shelf lists. These lists were made because books were then valuable property; also, they served as checklists against loss or theft, or in other cases, books were listed to commemorate donations made to the monastery (Thompson, 1939).

In larger collections, other techniques were employed to guide the user to the location of the literature. Pictures of authors on cupboards or walls would suggest the presence of related books, such as in the library of Isidor of Seville (530–636 AD) (Rovelstad, 1976).

A common practice was to use letters to designate the press and large Roman numerals to designate the shelf. The location of each volume was then indicated by a smaller Roman numeral. Sometimes, Roman letters were used to designate the press, and letters for the shelf (Thompson, 1939).

In the Augustinian House of Saint Victor (Paris), the desks were arranged in three rows and marked with triple series of letters.

The first row was marked: A, B, C
The second row: AA, BB, CC

The third row: AAA, BBB, CCC

To each of these letters were appended the numbers 1, 2, 3, to show the position of the required volume. It is not clear whether the numbers also appeared on the tables (there were 58 tables in the library), or only in the catalog that was prepared by Claude de Grandrue, one of the monks, in 1513.

(Clark, 1902)

From the thirteenth century onward, different colors were sometimes employed in labeling. Thus the books at Altenzelle, which were distributed among 36 desks, used red for theology, green for medicine, and black for law (Thompson, 1939).

During the Middle Ages, a common classification was between Christian works and Greek and Roman secular works.

From the catalogs of the library of Saint Martin's Priory of Dover (1389), we know that the library was divided into nine sections (classes), each marked by an alphabetical letter, including:

A   Bibles and commentaries
B   Sentences (legal rulings), historia, scholastica
C   Sermons and theological works
F   Civil and canon law
H   Logic, philosophy, rhetoric, medicine, chronicles, romances
I   Poetry, grammar, dictionaries

Each of these classes represented a book press and each was divided into seven grades (shelves), which were marked by Roman numerals. The numbering of the shelves began from the bottom and proceeded upward, so that the bottom shelf was marked I, the second II, and so on up to VII. In addition, the books of the library were all marked on each leaf with Arabic numerals (Norris, 1939) so as to facilitate the ascertaining of their content (Clark, 1902).

In every cathedral library, as well as in large monasteries, there were three different collections: (a) the main collection; (b) the service collection; and (c) the school library (known as the "little library" and used for instruction) (Thompson, 1939).

Book arrangement in the monasteries usually began with the Bible, then the Church Fathers, theologians, antique authors, and finally the liberal arts. In the tenth century, the old Carolinian monastery of Lorsch had a remarkable arrangement. First were entered liturgical works, then: Old and New Testaments; historical and geographical books; theological and patristic writings; Lives of Saints; and poetry (Thompson, 1939).

In the catalog of Prufening (1158), from which the first pages are lacking, the order was: biblical books (in a chronological sequence); the "old fathers"; Bede; Alcuin; Rabanus Maurus; great German ecclesiastics of the ninth and tenth centuries; and French theologians (Thompson, 1939).

In the catalog of Saint Maximin in Trier, which is of the eleventh or twelfth century, the order was: Bible and its parts; Augustiniani Libri; Ieronimiani Libri; Ambrosiani Libri; Gregoriani Libri; and Bedani Libri. Other writers of the epoch of each of these latter authors were included under these headings (Thompson, 1939).

The catalog of the books at the Abbey of Meaux in Holderness, founded in about the mid-twelfth century, was compiled in about 1396 and gives information on how the books were arranged. The presses in the Abbey's church mainly contained service books. In the common press in the cloister, "on the shelf over the door," were four Psalters; and on the top shelf, "the highest shelf opposite," there were 36 volumes. Then there were 11 groups of books, each containing, on average, 25 volumes. It is possible that each group represented one shelf. Each shelf was marked with letters of the alphabet, for a total of 316 books (Clark, 1902; Norris, 1939).

A list of books of the Notre Dame Cathedral (Église Cathédrale de Notre Dame) (Paris, 1297) arranged the books by subject: Textes de l'écriture Sainte avec ou sans commentaires (sacred books); Commentateurs sacrés (sacred books with commentary); Liturgie (liturgy); Théologiens (theology); Sermonnaires (sermons); Philosophie (philosophy); Histoire (history); Mélanges (miscellaneous) (Franklin, 1867).

As the libraries grew, arrangement became more standardized, often including seven classes:

(1) Archives;
(2) Scriptural texts and commentaries;
(3) Constitutions;
(4) Council and Synodal proceedings;
(5) Homilies and epistles of Fathers;
(6) Lectionaries;
(7) Legends of martyrdom.

When there was secular material as well, it was classified by the recognized liberal arts: grammar, rhetoric, logic, arithmetic, geometry, music, and astronomy (Thompson, 1939).

The medieval university collections were shelved according to the universities' disciplines. The library at the college endowed by Robert de Sorbonne (1250) in Paris set the pattern for others. Its catalog of 1290 was arranged by: Trivium (grammar, rhetoric and dialectic); Quadrivium (arithmetic, geometry, music, and astronomy); and the four faculties of the college: Theology, Medicine, Law, and Philosophy (Franklin, 1875). Within each group, there was a rough arrangement according to the first letter of the author's name. This practice became common in the college and university libraries. Thus in the Bodleian Library in the early seventeenth century, the books were divided according to the four university faculties: Theology, Medicine, Law, and the Arts. The books were then divided by size: folio, quarto, octavo. Within the subject division the books were arranged on the shelves in alphabetical order by the first letter of the authors' surnames (Norris, 1939; Frost, 1976). This rule still held in cases where several items were bound together. The book was then placed according to the surname of the first author (Norris, 1939).

Gabriel Naudé (1600–53), a French librarian in the courts of kings and churchmen, among them Cardinal Richelieu and Cardinal Mazarin, offered in his book *Advice on Establishing a Library* (1627) his views on book arrangement: "Books are put there for no other reason than to be serviceable as need arises. This, however, is impossible unless they be classified and arranged according to subject matter" (Naudé, [1627] 1950, p. 65). Naudé believed that to place all books under the three classes and principal headings Morals, Science, and Devotion was not sufficient. Instead he suggested a more detailed categorization into: Theology, Medicine, Jurisprudence, History, Philosophy, Mathematics, Humanities, and so on, each of which should be classified with subheadings according to its several divisions: "for example, in theology all the Bibles should be placed first, in the order of their languages; next to these the Councils, Synods, Decrees, Canons; after these, the Fathers, Greek, and Latin; then the commentators, scholastics, learned men of various schools, and historians; and finally, the heretics" (Naudé, [1627] 1950, p. 65).

For dealing with each field of learning, Naudé advised the following precautions:

> The first, that the most universal and ancient always take precedence; the second, that the interpreters and commentators be placed apart and sorted according to the order of the books which they explain; the third, that the special treatises follow the order and arrangement which their subject matter should occupy among the arts and sciences; the fourth and last, that all books of similar designation and the same subject matter be most precisely classified and set in the places assigned them.
>
> (Naudé, [1627] 1950, p. 66)

Buzás (1986), in his study of the history of the German library, notes that during the early modern period most practical classifications were by faculty, with contemporary modifications. The main medieval classes of theology, law, and medicine were preserved and among the liberal arts, different disciplines in diverse relationships were emphasized as main classes. Buzás discerned three basic combinations:

(1) the equal placement of all disciplines of the Trivium and Quadrivium, as well as history, geography, theology, law, and medicine (this was Conrad Gesner's classification of 1565);

(2) equal placement of theological disciplines, while law, medicine, and the artistic-humanistic subjects were reduced (this was the arrangement of Trefler, 1560, and of Clement, 1628);

(3)   the subordination of the artistic-humanistic subjects under the main classes of philosophy, history, and philology (and sometimes mathematics) and their equal placement with theology, law, and medicine (this was the arrangement of Leibniz, 1718).

In the seventeenth century the library of the Collège Mazarin was located in six halls, each containing different subjects. In the first hall, books on philosophy, law (mainly civic law), and theology were placed; in the second, books in the sciences (chemistry, natural history, medicine); in the third, Bibles; in the fourth, manuscripts; in the fifth, canon law and politics; and in the sixth, books by Luther and Calvin (Franklin, 1867).

Late in the seventeenth century a detailed classified arrangement, already popular in small libraries, spread to large ones. With the eighteenth century, book arrangement became more systematic; this was the century of encyclopedic thought and the Age of Enlightenment. In the early eighteenth century, the Sion College Library was classified by subject:

A	Bibles, Concordances
B	Liturgies
C	Rabbinical authors
D–E	Commentaries on the Bible
F	Expositors of the Scriptures and writings of Quakers, Anabaptists, Socinians, etc.
G–H	Greek and Latin Fathers with translations
I	Ecclesiastical and Civil Law
K	Councils, Canons, Convocations
L	Works of the Old Schoolmen, and the modern scholastic writers
M	Casuists, Catechisms
N	Controversies between Papists and Protestants
O	Preachers
P–Q	Miscellaneous Divinity
R	Medicine, Botany, Chirurgery, Anatomy, Chemistry
S	Ecclesiastical and Monastic History, Legends, Lives of the Saints

T	Ancient and modern History of the Greeks, Romans, etc.
U	History of England, Scotland, and Ireland, Political History, Biography
W	General History, Geography, Chronology
X	Philosophy
Y	Philology
Z	English, French, and Italian Philology
AB	Miscellaneous: Heraldry, Military Art, Hunting, Cookery, Country Life, Gardening
EB	Miscellaneous: Coins, Magic, Witchcraft, Demonology
IB	Dictionaries on all subjects
O	Mathematics, Astronomy, Architecture, Music, Optics
UB	Catalogues of public libraries

This is not a classification in the ordinary sense; the notation does not represent subjects, but particular book presses. The five groups at the end (AB, EB, IB, OB, UB) were actually overstock, which had to be put together because of lack of shelving (Norris, 1939).

The list of subjects in the Sainte-Geneviève Library in the late eighteenth century was quite detailed:

Bibles without commentaries
Bibles with commentaries
Liturgy
Councils, Synod constitution
Church Fathers
Theology (Catholic and heretic)
Canon Law
Civil Law
Geography, Travels, Chronology
History of the Church
History of the Empire
History of Modern Italy
History of France

History of Germany
History of the North Countries
History of Great Britain and Ireland
History of Spain and Portugal
Miscellaneous: Biographies, Periodicals, Catalogs
Philosophy
Natural History
Anatomy, Botany, Pharmacy, Chemistry, Medicine
Mathematics
Grammar, Rhetoric, Oratory
Poetry
Philology, Literary Critics
(Antiquities) Medals, Sport
Maps
Others books (shelved separately)
Manuscripts

(Franklin, 1867)

In those days there were two obstacles to a strict, systematic arrangement of books: the volumes that had unrelated items bound together, and the differences in the size of books. Since books in this period (the sixteenth century onward) had extreme differences in size, between folios and sixteenths, the appeal of an externally decorative organization was incompatible with an internal systematic arrangement (Buzás, 1986). Generally, the systematic arrangement ran in four parallel rows of formats shelved next to or above one another. Strict classification, such as in the Court Library of Vienna, was the exception (Buzás, 1986).

During the nineteenth century many new universities were established, new disciplines were created, academic communities more than doubled in size, and libraries could not cope with the numbers of new books and greater demands for their service. The addition of new books necessitated a constant shifting of the books on the shelves, changes in the catalog, and hence backlogs of unprocessed books.

One solution was to abandon the subject arrangement on the shelves, especially since the bulk of the collections was now closed to the public and the goal was more economical storage arrangements such as grouping the books by size, or by chronological order. The ideal of paralleling classification and shelves was abandoned. The books were arranged according to any arbitrary criterion such as size or accession number, and classification became a separate concept.

Most European libraries had closed stacks; in addition, there was a traditional suspicion in Europe of subject analysis or classification. Panizzi did not believe the subject catalog could answer the needs of the library, although he agreed that an alphabetical subject index should supplement the main author catalog. The distrust arose from the assumption that knowledge changes and cannot be expressed in fixed classification systems. These were regarded as inefficient and obsolete. Books were shelved in broadly defined subject groups. Under Panizzi, the British Museum collection was shelved in 650 sections. The Bibliothèque Nationale in Paris closed its stacks and started to shelve the books in the order of acquisition. This was the practice in all large libraries under the central control of the French government, and the municipal libraries followed suit. Book collections were grouped by size, and then placed according to the sequence of acquisition (Rovelstad, 1976).

The German libraries divided their materials into subject groups, then according to size, and then by accession number. Dr F. Rullmann, librarian of the University of Freiburg, asserted in 1874 that the most convenient way to place books on the shelves was from left to right, beginning from the lower shelves, and to have every book numbered. This numbering should not be continuous through a whole library, but merely through a division, since very high numbers, especially in large libraries, would cause considerable inconvenience (United States Bureau of Education, 1876, p. xxiii). The library of the Academy Nauk in Leningrad was arranged in 14 groups.

American libraries used a different approach. Most of them believed that classification schemes were logical arrangements, valid and efficient regardless of time and space. Most collections were smaller than in Europe; this prevented conflict between bibliographic and bibliothecal needs. From the start, most collections retained a broad subject order on the shelves (Hyman, 1982).

In nineteenth-century American libraries, the method of arrangement of the catalog did not consider how the books were arranged on the shelves. Books were usually given a fixed location and were arranged by different criteria: size, broad subject area, order of acquisition, alphabet, or a combination of these (Ranz, 1964). When books in libraries were first arranged in classes no one scheme was in general use, and almost every librarian formulated one of his own (Bostwick, 1917).

The need for classification was especially great with respect to collections that were open to the public. Poole (1876, p. 492) remarked that "A large library needs a more minute classification than a small library, and a library of reference [needs a more minute classification] than one of circulation." Bostwick (1917, p. 153) also pointed out: "Classification thus aids the open shelf reader directly and the closed-shelf reader indirectly through shelf arrangement as even with closed shelves classified shelf arrangement is of great aid to the assistant, whom it enables to answer questions regarding the available resources of the library."

Poole (1876) gave an example of a limited number of subjects:

History, biography, voyages and travels, poetry and drama, English miscellanies, English prose fiction, juveniles, polygraphy, collected works of English and American authors, German literature, French literature, Spanish literature, Italian literature, etc., language and rhetoric, fine and practical arts, natural history, physics and natural science, political and social science, education, religion, law, medicine, and serials.

(p. 492)

He explained that "In arranging the books under these general classes, each class must be further subdivided." As for the shelves, he noted that "ample space should be left for works in every department, and no bookcase should have more than half the books it will contain" (p. 493). In those days fixed location was still in use, and Poole suggested marking each book with its shelf mark. This involved designating the cases by letters, numbering the shelves in each case, and numbering the works consecutively as they stood on the shelves. By this plan, the shelf mark "A, 4,

10–2" would mean "Case A, 4th shelf, 10th work, 2nd vol."

In the circulating library the cases were designated by letters; the books in each case were given a numerical order, and sufficient numbers were reserved for the insertion of future acquisitions in their proper classified position. The books, here, did not stand permanently on any particular shelf, but in a fixed numerical order.

The next stage in the endeavor of intellectual arrangement of the shelf was the development of more detailed classification systems, as proposed by Dewey with his decimal system of classification, which in its first edition of 1876 already numbered one thousand subjects; and by Cutter in his *Expansive Classification*, according to which the Library of Congress classification system was developed.

The development of detailed classification systems arose from the growth of collections and from the transition to the open shelf. Cutter clarifies this point in *Expansive Classification*:

> The reason for classification is that people often wish to see many books on a subject at once either in order to read the whole literature of a subject, or that they may examine it and select the best works. A classified arrangement is also sometimes an assistance in finding a book whose author's name has been forgotten, tho [sic] its subject is remembered. It also frequently enables one to get a book without consulting the catalog to find where it is placed.
>
> (Cutter, 1891–93, p. 4)

He added: "The gain from classification is greatest in libraries which admit visitors to the shelves."

Dewey asserted in 1879 that there were four systems of order available:

> Order of size, accession, author's name, and subject. To arrange by title was impractical; by date was of use simply in cases in the nature of volumes or serials, as in arranging an author's works or showing the development of a science. A size and accession were found of use only as modifiers of the main system; we are left to choose from only two arrangements, viz., by author's names or by subjects. Order by author's name is alphabetical order. Several large libraries used it – this does not prove that it is a good system.

It is without any doubt the only system of finding any book without catalog or index, and with only the information generally possessed by the readers.

(Dewey, 1879, pp. 191–2)

Since he rejected arrangement according to authors, he felt this only left the alternative of arrangement according to subjects. Dewey ([1926] 1965) explained that his search for a new method of arranging books and catalogs arose from the fact that catalogs, made at great cost, soon became antiquated, and the method used for shelving involved frequent rearrangement, renumbering, and re-marking of books.

A classification system is the systematic arrangement by subject of books and other material on shelves, or of catalog and index entries, in the manner which is most useful to those who read or who seek a definite piece of information. Classification is not only the general grouping of items for location or identification purposes. It is also their arrangement in some sort of rational order so that the main relationships of the items in question can be ascertained (Maltby, 1975). As Svenonius (1981) pointed out, classification, at least in the United States, has been used to facilitate browsing of books on shelves.

Close classification became a topic of controversy almost as soon as open access was introduced (Hyman, 1972). Dewey pointed out in 1879 that the only question that arises is where to stop dividing by subject. He remarked that "the best arrangement of a library is that which shows quickest what it contains. All my experience and study on this question tends strongly towards close classification on the shelves, leaving the rest to the catalog" (Dewey, 1879, pp. 192–3).

In the "Introduction" to the 10th edition ([1926] 1965) of his *Decimal Classification*, Dewey wrote: "Subdivisions are made in such a way that one may uze all, or any part and ignore the rest without difficulty or confuzion, thus allowing each to uze minute subdivisions where he wishes or needs them, without being forst into refinements in subjects where he has few books or litl interest [Dewey's spelling]."

Ranganathan also dealt with this issue in his book *Elements of*

Library Classification (1962), which was first published in India in 1945. He maintained that "the librarian classifies to uncover to himself, in order to make it readily available to readers everything that a library has on any subject – the resources uncovered by minute classification are extremely important to know" (p. 150).

Some libraries, to make things easier for the user, give only the first three or four of Dewey's numbers. Instead of close classification, they provide a broader classification. This is a widespread practice in public and school libraries, but sometimes is also used in college libraries – for example, Lamont Undergraduate Library at Harvard, or the Surrey County Library, England, in which most class numbers extend to only one digit beyond the decimal point, with a maximum of two digits where absolutely necessary. Some topics carry an alphabetical subset, for example, "796.3 CRI" for cricket or "796.3 GOL" for golf.

Along with these general classification systems, to which have been added the Library of Congress Classification System, UDC (Universal Decimal Classification), Ranganathan's Colon Classification, and Bliss's Bibliographic Classification, other shelf-classification methods exist, such as:

- Shelving by title, which is commonly used for shelving periodicals and magazines, each periodical then being arranged by date;
- Shelving by author, which is the common arrangement for fiction;
- Shelving by the target reading group – e.g., adult literature, children's literature, juvenile literature;
- Shelving by languages;
- Shelving by the material format or medium, e.g., manuscripts, periodicals, books, audio material, videocassettes, kits.

In other words, different shelf-arrangement principles exist and one may find a number of different types of arrangement in one library. Some arrangements are according to the material format and medium:

- Reference materials are usually separately housed in a designated area.

- In most libraries fiction is separate from nonfiction.
- Most libraries use separate housing for newspapers, magazines, and unbound periodicals.
- Vertical file collections of pamphlets, clippings, and folded maps are separately and differently shelved.
- Works of art for lending are stored separately.
- Audio materials are shelved in special cabinets, arranged by the genre of music, and then by the composer or performer.
- Videocassettes are shelved separately, by genre or the film's title.
- Microfilms, mainly of newspapers and serials, are kept in a special cabinet.

In many libraries books may be removed from their regular sequence in order to be included in a display about a certain subject or person, or simply because they are new and public attention needs to be drawn to them.

There are also arrangements that are based on categories of clients. In its early days, the public library oriented itself to certain types of customers – adults, city dwellers, literati. Gradually these target groups were broadened. By the late nineteenth century, one of the main groups of book borrowers was children. Catering for this group entailed: acquisition of children's books; allocation of space in the library – a separate corner or room; and special services for children provided by specially trained librarians.

In 1885, in New York City, the first experiment with giving library services to children was made. The collection of children's books was transferred from branch to branch, then finally closed. In 1896 there were separate rooms for children in a number of libraries, including ones in Boston, Cambridge, and Brooklyn. In other libraries, special areas were allocated to children; this was done in Buffalo and Cleveland (Bostwick, 1917).

The children's collection is normally in a designated area of the library; it is then divided between children's fiction and children's nonfiction; children's fiction is usually then further subdivided according to grade and reading levels, at least separating the picture books and "easy reading books." Sometimes material for parents and adults working with children will also be found in the children's section.

Although it is common to put fiction books in alphabetical order by their authors' surnames, in some children's rooms from an early period, fiction was classified and shelved with nonfiction; thus, a historical tale of the French Revolution would be found with histories of that period. Bostwick (1917) tells about at least one library in the United States in which books in the children's room were arranged by accession number, without classification order, so that the users would be more likely to select nonfiction.

Only in the twentieth century did the realization develop that young adults have a separate subculture and needs of their own, and libraries began to provide services to this age group. Here, too, this took the form of allocating a corner or even a separate room with a special collection intended to suit the interests of adolescents. The first library that developed special services for adolescents was the city library of Cleveland, which in 1925 opened the Robert Louis Stevenson Room for Young Adults. After World War II there was a rapid spread of such facilities (Wheeler, 1981).

Awareness of the special needs of the elderly, and the creation of special collections and services for them in libraries, emerged much later. The earlier library had oriented its services toward youth and productive workers; at that time the elderly were an insignificant proportion of the population. However, because of the sharp increase in life expectancy, which changed the elderly into a larger group with greater social, economic, and political salience, libraries appreciated the need to pay special attention to them. Professional services for the elderly actually began in the 1940s but became widespread only after World War II, with better levels of education (including among elderly people): senior citizens have increased leisure time for reading and other recreational activities; modern reading aids have enabled many more people to read; and the grouping of older people in nursing and retirement homes has made it much easier to reach them and to offer them special services (Brown, 1971).

The first service for elderly people was provided in the

Cleveland Public Library in 1946, and was called "Live Long and Like It." A club in the library encouraged members over 60 years old to remain active, and offered various programs. Other libraries emulated this service, among them libraries in Boston, Brooklyn, Chicago, Detroit, Washington, and elsewhere. Many libraries, mainly in the United States and Western Europe, maintained a separate collection of books in large print.

Opposition, from a pedagogical viewpoint, to defining readers according to their age, led in some cases to the eschewing of such categories. Certain combinations of material designated for children and for adults were tried in Ontario and California, for example, but encountered much criticism from the public (Hyman, 1982).

In later years the notion of combining collections for different age groups has gained prominence in public librarianship. This approach is closely connected to the organizational philosophy known as the "generalist" approach, among whose proponents is the Baltimore County Public Library. In 1976, Baltimore County Public Library combined the adults' and children's librarians into one working team. Adult and juvenile nonfiction collections were interfiled. A general browsing area was created with separate fiction collections for adults, young adults, and children as well as a picture-book collection (Babikow, 1985).

Combinations of fiction and nonfiction books for adults have also been tried. Bostwick (1917) described a "ribbon" arrangement of fiction, in which fiction is placed on shelves around the room, with nonfiction classes above and below it. The expectation is that many users who read only fiction will in this way be attracted to nonfiction books as well. In addition, sometimes very practical criteria, rather than theoretical or pedagogical concepts, determine the arrangement of books. Even in our day, it is sometimes the size of the document that decides where it will be placed. Books of exceptional size are shelved separately in most libraries even today. Sometimes they are placed on the lowest shelf of the bookcase and sometimes in a separate area of the library.

The uncertainty about which classification system best suits readers has still not been resolved; different strategies are found in different libraries. Thus, some libraries integrate age groups and materials where, in the past, separation was practiced. For example, the Surrey County Library (England) integrated, within each nonfiction category, the adult nonfiction stock, children's nonfiction stock (except "easy readers"), and reference stock (but not quick reference) – all including oversize books. Periodicals were located close to their parent categories when practical (Ainley and Totterdell, 1982).

Despite the fact that general classification systems have been absorbed by libraries and are in wide international use, the uncertainty and the search for new approaches have continued. Since the 1940s, shelf-arrangement systems have been sought that are better suited to readers' interests. Many libraries in Britain, mainly public ones, have been criticized on the ground that traditional classification systems such as the Dewey system, in creating a logical set of relationships between subjects, fail to take account of changing interests. Thus, it is charged that books appear together on shelves yet have no relationship other than a formal, academic one (Ainley and Totterdell, 1982).

Sawdridge and Favret (1982) questioned whether classification was worth the effort and asserted that surveys showed a complete mismatch between the service offered and the pattern of public library use. They maintained that the library is organized for people who know fairly exactly what they want.

In the early 1980s, Sawdridge and Favret (1982) carried out experiments with readers' interest groups in a branch library in the Bexley (England) library service. Instead of using the alphabetical sequence by broad groups, they rearranged the materials. The nonfiction was arranged in broad categories, and they reduced the stock by 25 percent to allow more room for face-out display. Issues for nonfiction increased 30 percent and reader reactions were generally favorable.

Already in the 1930s, Micklewright (1935) suggested considering the public point of view when deciding on the arrangement of any collection of books. He advocated the categorization of fiction to aid those who do not know what they want.

In 1976, the public library in Cheshire, England, placed its stock into 22 different interest categories; a finite allocation of shelving with a fixed location was given to each category. The subcategories were:

General textbook
Biography and history
Countryside and travel
Home and garden
Society (including religion)
Recreation
Arts and crafts
Fiction – which in turn was subdivided into:
    Romance, Western, Science Fiction, Historical, General, Adventure, Thriller, Short Stories
Large print – Fiction and nonfiction [a distinction by the material format]
Young people [a distinction by clients' age group]
                                        (Ainley and Totterdell, 1982)

At the public libraries in Cambridgeshire, England, the collection was divided into three sections: Fiction, Nonfiction, and Fiction and Nonfiction Combined.

Fiction categories were: Western; Romance; General Fiction; Family Stories; Historical; Short Stories.

Nonfiction categories were: Language and Literature; Britain; Rest of the World; Science, Mathematics, and Computers; People in Society; Philosophy and Religion; Man, Machine, and Invention; Country Life; Gardening and Nature; Animals and Pets; Hobbies, Domestic Arts and Crafts; Family and Health; Food and Drinks; The Arts; Biography; Games and Sports; Local Studies; Large Print.

The Fiction and Nonfiction Combined categories were: Crime, Mysteries, and Detection; Adventure and Spy; The Sea; The Unknown (Science Fiction, Fantasy, Ghost, Astrology).

This approach was first implemented in the early 1940s in the

Detroit Public Library. This library devised the "Reader Interest Classification" (RIC), which was designed to serve readers' interests with two kinds of categorization: (1) browsing, for those readers who have no fixed need in mind but are stimulated to recognize their interests by the category; and (2) subject, for those aware of their interest in a certain field who can associate it with definite subjects but not with related interests (Dunkin, 1969).

In 1959, the Detroit Public Library used 14 categories: Background Reading; The Arts; Current Affairs; People and Places; The Bright Side; Sports; Hobbies; Personal Living; Your Family; Your Home; Group Activities; Business; Technology; and Information. A category might have several subheadings. Under each subheading, books were arranged alphabetically. All this amounted to broad rather than close classification, with no attempt to bring together related topics that might be separated by the Dewey classification system (Dunkin, 1969).

At the Hoddesdon Library in Hertfordshire, England, a distinction was made between a Family collection and a Subject collection. The Family category included materials for recreation such as: novels, magazines and newspapers, large-print books, children's books, some nonfiction subjects (cookery, gardening, pets, sports, biographies, car manuals, theater, travel), and a children's area. The Subject library included nonfiction subjects such as: sciences, languages, law, religion, psychology, electronics, and economics (Ainley and Totterdell, 1982).

In some public libraries, paperback collections are divided into interest browsing categories (Hyman, 1982). A similar division into interest categories is sometimes found in the children's collection. In a junior high school library in San Jose, California, the librarian grouped the fiction collection (which contained 3,000 titles) into eight categories: Story collection; Fantasy; Sports; Mystery and suspense; Girls' stories; Science fiction; Historical fiction; General fiction. Colors were used to designate the categories.

Summary

The division into types of collection began in ancient times with the distinction between temple libraries and palace libraries. In each of these libraries there was some sort of system for arrangement of the tablets and the papyrus.

In the Alexandrian library's *Pinakes*, there was a detailed system of arrangement. We know at least of the following subjects: Poetry, Law, Philosophy, History, Rhetoric, and Medicine. Some of these subjects were further subdivided into subtopics. This categorization of subjects in the Alexandrian library is indicative of the size of some of the Greek and Hellenistic libraries.

In Roman libraries, a distinction was made first of all between collections of Greek and of Roman books. In the Middle Ages, when collections were much smaller than in ancient times, consisting of only a few dozen or at most a few hundred books, and generally were concentrated in monasteries, there was no longer a need for systematic, elaborate, detailed arrangement of books. In this period a distinction was commonly made between sacred and secular books, most of the secular ones being Greek or Roman.

Only in the late Middle Ages with the growth of collections, and the rise of cathedral and university libraries, did the division of collections by subject matter begin. Secular books were divided into categories of the recognized liberal arts. In university libraries, a classification was commonly made according to fields of study, mainly theology, law, and medicine.

Incunabulum books were characterized by different sizes, which sometimes led to the arrangement of books in libraries according to size. Arranging books according to size and according to university disciplines continued into the seventeenth century.

In the seventeenth and eighteenth centuries, the further growth of collections led to the use of a larger number of subject categories, sometimes up to 20 or more in a library. At the same time, the size of some collections and the fact that some books were bound together prevented the strict, systematic arrangement of books.

In the nineteenth century, the growth both in the size of collections and in the number of clients of libraries led to two contradictory developments. On the one hand, many collections were closed to direct access by the public, thus allowing books to be arranged in whatever way was convenient, and not necessarily by subject. On the other hand, in the United States toward the end of the century, closed classification systems were developed. Dewey, in the first edition of his landmark book in 1876, proposed one thousand subjects rather than the several dozen broad categories commonly used up to that time.

Since then, the general classification systems have undergone many elaborations and additions, and today they comprise tens of thousands of subjects. A hundred years after the establishment of these systems, this situation has led back to a search, in public and school libraries, for broad categories that the public would both take an interest in and be capable of understanding.

We have now entered the electronic age, and though we are somewhat bewildered by different prognostications, it is clear that various materials will gradually be transferred to the electronic medium. This development will call into question the usefulness of classification systems for intellectual arrangement of the library's contents, intended to enable clients to wander and browse among shelves that are arranged according to subjects in which they are likely to take an interest.

The question is whether, in the virtual library, wandering among bookshelves will occur as it has since ancient times, or whether sophisticated consolidation systems will replace the need for systematic arrangement of the documents even on the computer screen.

4

Access to the Shelves

It is not known whether libraries in ancient times provided access to their collections. Even if they did, it was certainly for a very restricted public. The fact that the two-chamber library of Assur-bani-pal, king of Nineveh, was accessible from the entrance to the palace has led scholars to speculate that people from outside the palace may also have had access to the library.

Harris (1995) suggested that the library of Assur-bani-pal was open to scholars, both official and unofficial. As Clark (1902) queries: "Does not the position of these two rooms, easily accessible from the entrance to the palace, shew [*sic*] that their contents might be consulted by persons who were denied admission to the more private apartments?" (p. 4). Weitemeyer (1956) cited a text that appeared on a tablet, from Erech, containing a description of a town in Babylon, which showed that a select group did have access to the library: "He who is learned shall withhold [it] for the benefit of him who is [also] learned; he who has no learning shall not see [it]" (p. 230).

In some of the Egyptian temples there were two libraries, one for the use of all who could read, and the other, which contained theological works, for a select circle of high priests (Harris, 1995). However, this does not necessarily mean that the persons who were allowed to enter these reading rooms were granted direct access to the documents, which were stored in cases or on special shelves.

It is known that there were private libraries in Greece. Aristotle was probably the earliest private citizen who had a library. We know of some other private libraries, for example, those of

Nococrates of Cyprus, and of Clearchus of Heraclea. Although these were private, undoubtedly at least some of them were open to scholars (Thompson, [1940] 1962). In Rome as well there were many private libraries. Some of them were owned by cultured individuals, but there were also *nouveaux riches* who aspired to maintain book collections.

Both in Greece and in Rome there were public libraries, and they, of course, were open at least to some of the local public. The first public library in Athens was established in 330 BC in order to maintain authorized copies of the popular tragedies of Aeschylus, Sophocles, and Euripides. The first public library in ancient Rome was founded by Asinius Pollio after his Dalmatian triumph in 37 BC (Thompson, [1940] 1962).

In the Greek and Roman libraries there was usually a clear distinction between the reading room and the storage area, and the libraries were used for additional purposes: they were popular spots for conversation or meditation, and also for public meetings and lectures. Rhetorical contests were often held in them. Augustus held meetings of the Senate in the Palatine library (Thompson, 1940). According to Aulus Gellius, the libraries of Polycrates, tyrant of Samos, and of Peisistratus, tyrant of Athens (sixth century BC), were accessible to all who cared to use them. Clark (1902), however, doubted the veracity of this.

Even if some members of the public were given access to the libraries, it should be recalled that in antiquity books were stored using what we now call the closed-shelf system. Books were placed in cases (presses), in pigeonholes, and sometimes on shelves. In other words, this was a densely packed storage for the purpose of maintaining the books, and the public was not allowed free access to them.

In the Middle Ages, books were maintained by monasteries. The collections were extremely small, and used mainly by residents of the monasteries. The "Customs of the Augustinian Order" give a picture of the common practice in the monasteries: "books are to be kept at hand for daily use, whether for singing or reading, ought to be in some common place, to which all the brethren can have easy access for inspection, and selection of anything which seems to be suitable. The books, therefore, ought not to be carried away into chambers, or into corners outside the Cloister or the Church" (Clark, 1902, p. 61). However, the lending of books by the monasteries to persons outside, on adequate security, began at a very early date. The Rila Monastery in Bulgaria established a library shortly after its founding in the tenth century; this library loaned books, though on a limited scale (Khristova, 1983).

According to the rules of the Benedictine libraries, books could be borrowed by outside people. In the Customs of the Benedictine House at Abingdon in Berkshire, England, from the late twelfth century, it was stated: "The precentor [librarian] cannot sell, or give away, or pledge any books; nor can he lend any except on deposit of a pledge, of equal or greater value than the book itself ... However he may not lend except to neighbouring churches, or to persons of conspicuous worth" (Clark, 1902, pp. 58–9). In the sixteenth century the libraries of the Benedictine House of Saint-Germain-des-Prés (Paris) and of Saint Victor (Paris) were open to all visitors on certain days of the week (Clark, 1902).

The 1391 catalog of Durham Cathedral Library gives evidence of borrowing. Frequently against entries there are such notes as "Accomodatur J. Whixlay" or "Stockton habet," indicating that books had been borrowed by individuals named J. Whixlay and Stockton. Such phrases as *"Est vetus liber"* or *"Ponitur in libraria"* are scattered throughout the catalog (Norris, 1939, p. 63).

Very similar instructions to those of the Benedectine libraries were found in the Customs of the Augustinian Order in England as well as in France and Belgium:

> Nor ought the librarian himself to lend books unless he receive a pledge of equal value; and then he ought to enter on his roll the name of the borrower, the title of the book lent, and the pledge taken. The larger and more valuable books he ought not to lend to anyone, known or unknown, without permission of the Prelate.
>
> (Clark, 1902, p. 61)

The practice of lending became common, and was indeed enjoined on monks as a duty by their ecclesiastical superiors. In 1212 a council that met in Paris promulgated the following decree:

We forbid those who belong to a religious Order to formulate any vow against lending their books to those who are in need of them; seeing that to lend is enumerated among the principal works of mercy. After careful consideration, let some books be kept in the House for the use of brethren; others, according to the decision of the abbat, be lent to those who are in need of them.

(Clark, 1902, p. 64)

Clark (1902) even went so far as to call the monastic libraries the public libraries of the Middle Ages. We must recall, however, that some parts of collections could not be borrowed in any case, and that only very restricted categories of persons were allowed to borrow.

In addition, abbeys continually loaned books to each other, either for reading or for copying. Copying could be performed only if an exemplar was obtained from an external source; for example, we know that among the houses of the Carthusian Order, an inter-library loan system was employed. From the most important Carthusian collection in London, materials were loaned to other houses for copying. When a monk was to be transferred from London to another house, he would bring with him the requested manuscripts (Large, 1975).

Of the lists of books loaned by the London house to other houses during the fourteenth and fifteenth centuries, few are extant (Thompson, 1930). In 1343 the Hinton house lent about 20 books to another religious house; among them are listed: "Two books of Homilies, to be read in the refectory; The four Gospels; The Meditations of St Anselm; The life of John the Almoner; A treatise of Peter of Cluny; *Flores et magna glossa Psalterii*" (Thompson, 1930, p. 323). Such an inter-library loan system was not confined to national borders, but extended to the Continent. The movement of monks between England and the Continent became a means for the transfer of books (Large, 1975).

This practice of borrowing with security continued even with the establishment of the university libraries. The regulations of the Sorbonne Library state that books could be borrowed only with a pledge worth more than the value of the book. Such a pledge could be given in money, in gold, or by depositing another book. In the *Regestrum bibliothecae* of the Sorbonne University (fifteenth century), the names of doctors and students who borrowed books were inscribed as well as the books' titles and the sums of money paid as deposits (Franklin, 1867, p. 246). The principle of lending books to students under a pledge was also used by the Oxford and Cambridge universities – as early as the thirteenth century at Oxford. Since the books were precious possessions, heavy penalties were imposed for failing to return them, such as withdrawal of the right to borrow for a year; or even, if that was not effective, expulsion from studies.

From detailed instructions about maintenance of the libraries at Cambridge and Oxford, we learn that the books were to be kept in chests secured by locks; the chests could only be opened if a number of officials were present. These volumes could not be borrowed indiscriminately, but each scholar (Fellow) could choose the book he wanted and write a formal acknowledgment that he had received it; he was then obligated to return it or pay its value, under a severe penalty. Once a year, the whole collection was to be audited in the presence of the Master of the College and all of the Fellows.

The rules of the founder of Trinity Hall in Cambridge, William Bateman, state that the books not being borrowed were to be "kept in some safe room, to be assigned for the College Library, so that all the Scholars of the College may have common access to them" (Clark, 1902, p. 130). This arrangement at university libraries subsequently developed into a selection of books required for reference, and the chaining of them in the "Library chamber for the common use of the fellows" (Clark, 1902). That is, a portion of the books were set on desks, though chained; but essentially there was direct access at least to part of the collection. In the lectern system of storage, which was common during the Middle Ages, books were at first set directly on the desk, and afterward on shelves over the desk, fastened by chains to ensure that they would not disappear. This provided direct access, though to a small number of users, and only to some of the books.

The chains, which on the one hand enabled fastening of the books to the desks, on the other hand enabled the books to be used. The chains, then, were the technology that brought a change in library policy and the granting of direct access to books. They solved the problem of security – namely the fear of theft when users gained access by themselves to the books; in these times books were still hand-copied manuscripts and were extremely valuable. In the stall system as well, and later with the transition to the hall-type library, readers had direct access to the chained books.

During the Renaissance and the Baroque period, the owners of libraries usually allowed the use of their collections to people with whom they were familiar: but with the spread of education, a larger public began to demand access to the stored knowledge. When some libraries opened their doors to "the public" and one could enter them freely and without difficulty, the categories of users became larger.

During the fifteenth and sixteenth centuries, lending of books was permitted in the college libraries of the Ottoman Empire. In the Fatih Library (1470), a librarian was given the function of organizing and supervising the lending (Erünsal, 1984). In the deed of the Seyh Vefa Library, Istanbul (1485), the lending of books to well-known upper-class individuals was allowed without a deposit; middle- and lower-class people had to leave a deposit. Besides asking for a deposit, some library founders and owners limited the duration of a loan (from one month to one year). However, from the eighteenth century the lending of books in the Ottoman libraries was forbidden, because of losses of books that had been incurred (Erünsal, 1984).

During the sixteenth century there was still a fear of individuals who were unfamiliar to the library staff. According to the regulations of the Sorbonne (1531), a stranger was allowed to enter only if accompanied by a regular user of the library, and if closely observed while in the library (Franklin, 1867).

The Ambrosiana in Milano (1603) was the first large library to adopt a more liberal policy; it was followed by the Bodleian at Oxford (1612), the Mazarine in Paris (1643) (Rovelstad, 1976), and the library of the Augustinian Friars in Rome (Naudé, [1627] 1950). Since these libraries did not allow books to circulate, the books had to be used in the library rooms themselves. At the Bodleian Library the folio was chained to the desks, and accessible to all readers; the quartos and octavos were shelved apart and kept under lock and key (Norris, 1939).

Naudé, in his 1627 book *Advice on Establishing a Library*, suggested that the library should allow people to enter freely and that well-known persons of distinction should be permitted to carry a few, ordinary books to their own lodgings for up to three weeks on condition that they signed a document saying they had done so.

The Abbaye de Sainte-Geneviève library was opened to the public in 1710. However, entrance was allowed only to respectable people "volontiers l'entrée aux honnêtes gens qui la lui demandent" (Franklin, 1867, p. 79). In 1735 it was decided to open the library every day for a few hours, to enable established persons to borrow books. In 1759 the discrimination between people was abolished by a royal edict and everyone who desired to study was allowed in, though only during the restricted hours of two to five o'clock on Mondays, Wednesdays, and Fridays.

During the seventeenth and eighteenth centuries, the practice of chaining books gradually disappeared. Printed books were far cheaper than manuscripts, and far easier to duplicate, so that there was less and less rationale for chaining. For a long time, libraries remained relatively small and served limited groups of users who usually were known personally to the librarians. Thus in 1615 it was decided at the Sorbonne Library to unchain the books, though the chains were retained in case the policy was reversed, and indeed two years later the librarians were permitted to chain 12 volumes anew, among them three catalogs (Franklin, 1867).

Toward the end of the eighteenth century, however, the reader–book relationship was increasingly influenced by two main factors. First, to make studying more comfortable, small rooms were made available for reading purposes to more of the users in the larger libraries. These rooms were easily heated and allowed the librarians better observation of the readers. Secondly, there was a steady growth in the quantity of books, which required more efficient storage methods. The tendency was toward shelving in large multi-tier stacks with parallel ranges, close together to increase the storage capacity. Thus, a distinction between stacks and reading rooms gradually began to emerge.

Increasingly, the reading rooms became the only areas open to readers, whereas the stacks were closed, or sometimes open only to privileged users (Rovelstad, 1976). This tendency was further strengthened in the nineteenth century with the establishment of public libraries, which brought in a wide public not personally familiar to the librarians, and with the growth of the universities, which brought to the academic libraries a wide public of students.

Winsor (1876), the superintendent of the Boston Public Library, explained the separation of the readers from the books:

> The alcove system, arranged about a central area, where the books are also to be used, is to this day the most convenient plan where a collection is devoted to a small or solely scholarly use, and where, as is the case with scientific societies or other bodies of specialists, their members are allowed unrestricted access to the shelves. When we come to change the character of the library to that of a great collection to which multitudes have access, and but few are personally known to the librarians [it] involves the shutting out of the public from the shelves.
>
> (p. 466)

In academic libraries the collections were mostly closed to the students, although in reading rooms certain reference books were freely available. A survey of college libraries by Warren and Clark (1876) addressed the issue of access to collections. Their description of the Georgetown College Library reflected the situation in most academic libraries:

> The Library of Georgetown College, Georgetown, D.C. contains 28,000 volumes. Books are never loaned outside of the college. Students may visit the library to consult authorities, but they rarely have occasion to do so, as their own society libraries are well supplied with standard works, to which access can be had by them at any moment.
>
> (p. 72)

The description of the library at Wellesley (Massachusetts) College for young women, which was established in 1875, mentioned that "the cases for the books are all protected by glass doors" (p. 93). Robinson (1876) noted that "Dictionaries, cyclopaedias, gazetteers, maps, and other works of reference are best kept where every reader can have free and easy access to them during all library hours" (p. 510); however, "students are not allowed to take books from the shelves" (p. 519).

Sometimes the newspaper room was also open to the public. Winsor (1876) describes among the library areas a newspaper room that "should have conveniences for attendants to do the work of assorting and collating newspapers for the binder, and should have tables for consulting them" (p. 471).

In the conference of librarians held in London, October 2–5, 1877, at which many Americans were present, the majority, including Dewey, condemned the open-shelf approach. The American Library Association (ALA) held its first discussion on this issue in 1888. Most of those who spoke in favor of open shelves advocated only partial free access. However, a woman named Martha Nelson reported that the public library of Trenton, New Jersey, had for some time opened its shelves to the public (Bostwick, 1917).

Dewey (1879) himself, though uncertain at first, understood the importance of browsing and sampling the books. "No catalog ever did, ever will, or ever can take the place of the books themselves. The best work is done by seeing them together" (p. 193).

The classification system that Dewey developed was initially intended for the catalog. He very quickly, however, grasped its potential for shelf arrangement. In his introduction to the second edition of Dewey Decimal Classification (1885), he noted that the system had been devised for cataloging and indexing but had been found equally valuable for numbering and arranging books and pamphlets on the shelves.

Cutter (1886), too, favored direct access to books even though he also attributed great importance to the catalog:

> It is as true for the librarian as for the student that the best catalog is the books on the shelves. The catalog answers a different class of questions or answers the same questions in a different way. If it is well made, it comes nearer bringing everything together than the shelves can ever do; but it does not show the character of the books as well as does a glance at them or the mere sight of their

outsides to one who has seen them before. The difference is like that between textbooks and object teaching. In fact to the scholar a book on the shelves is worth two in the catalog.

(p. 180)

In a symposium held by the *Library Journal* in 1890, there was no mention of open access to shelves. Among the first to raise the issue was the humanist scholar James K. Hosmer who at an ALA conference in 1890 spoke about the value of research-browsing in open-shelf collections (Hosmer, 1890).

In a lecture in 1891, Thomas Wentworth Higginson lauded the "open-access" library as the "free library of the future" and mentioned large libraries that had open access, namely Cleveland and Columbus in Ohio, and the Boston Athenaeum. In the Free Library of Pawtucket, Rhode Island, the shelves were open as early as 1879.

The topic became controversial; librarians raised many arguments against free direct access to collections, especially regarding their security. The issue of extending library services to the "unknown public" generated controversies for several decades; many librarians were concerned about theft and misplacement. It was feared that direct access by people wandering freely among the books would overburden the library system because users would wear out the books more quickly with increased handling, and misplace them on the shelves. Misplacement might also lead to dissatisfied clients:

> Masses are impatient of delay and need to be served quickly in order to be kept happy; and to accomplish it the page who goes for a book must not be obliged to scan titles along a shelf, or series of shelves, but must find a book at once by its number in its proper place. Thus to insure a certainty of the book being in its place, it is necessary to exclude the public from the shelves for the reason that most prowlers among shelves do not restore books they have taken down to the exact place from which they took them.
>
> (Winsor, 1876, p. 466)

To these claims were added pedagogical arguments. Librarians in public libraries also feared, in certain periods, that direct access would lead to clients selecting inferior books, and believed that the choice of books should remain under the librarian's control. Librarians saw it as their task to direct patrons unfamiliar with literature to the best books. Cutter (1904) suggested that catalogs should call attention to the best books in order "to lay out courses of reading for that numerous class who are desirous of improving their minds, and are willing to spend considerable effort and time but know neither where to begin or how to go on" (p. 105).

From 1876 on, librarians concerned with their pedagogical duty warned against the hazards of unguided direct access. If it was not always possible to guide users, then attention should at least be paid to the quality of collections. Many believed, therefore, that a policy of careful acquisition was one way to cope with the situation, and many relied on authoritative buying guides.

Before the turn of the century, open shelves in large metropolitan libraries were unthinkable, with the exception of the Cleveland Public Library. This was the only large library reporting unrestricted access for all persons to all books at all times. William Howard Brett, the librarian there from 1884 to 1918, believed that patrons should be offered temptations (Conmy, 1975). The new plan for the library was introduced in April 1890, and a year later at the San Francisco ALA conference Brett reported that it had been successful and had increased the circulation (Bostwick, 1917).

Some other libraries allowed partial access to their collections. One such was the Minneapolis Free Public Library, which opened in 1889. The head of the library at that time, Herbert Putnam, granted "shelf permits" to several hundred persons pursuing special courses of reading or whose professional work involved special research. The shelf permits were given for periods extending from one day to one year, usually to people who could be relied on to observe the rules of the library ("Access to shelves", 1891).

In addition, the Minneapolis Public Library's reference reading room held nearly a thousand volumes of reference books to be used without a record. Also, all current newspapers and periodicals were placed in open cases or on tables in the reading room. The medical reading room and the patent room were open without restrictions ("Access to shelves", 1891). In the summer, in the quiet hours, the Minneapolis Public Library sometimes provided free access to the shelves; as a result, use increased by 50 percent during the summer. On the other hand, in the library branches, the access to collections was totally free; these libraries were small and had only small collections and few clients, most of them known to the librarians, and did not contain expensive academic reference books or rare books. Also, these branches aimed to stimulate their local communities intellectually.

At the Minneapolis Free Public Library, it was decided to differentiate and make a certain portion of the books freely accessible; if not all the time, at least for some hours, and if not to all people, at least to some (Putnam, 1891). Putnam's (1891) policy reflected his belief in the educational importance of exposure to books. "I cannot believe there is a librarian who has felt as a reader and would not himself be urgent for freedom of access. The problem is one of means" (p. 64).

At the Lake Placid (New York) conference of 1894, Dr Steiner of Baltimore reported on a survey of 105 libraries, which found that nearly all of them granted free access to a few reference books and many to nearly all such books (Bostwick, 1917). Most libraries restricted access to certain classes of books and some to certain hours. Of the libraries that allowed access to circulating books, the general verdict was against free access to fiction and juvenile books. Bostwick (1917) reported on six libraries that had tried free access and had abandoned it.

The Free Library of Philadelphia, which opened in 1894, gave entirely free access from the beginning; this lent the trend a great impetus. Open access had been common in small popular libraries, but was widely regarded as impracticable for larger institutions. Toward the end of the second decade of the twentieth century, Bostwick (1917) reported that all public libraries were divided into two categories: closed-shelf and open-shelf, or free access, libraries. Practically all small and medium-size libraries were at that time open-shelf.

Open access became universal in America in all but large city libraries, and even in these there was usually an open-shelf room containing many thousands of volumes. In children's reading rooms, of course, open access became the common practice.

The rise of open access in public libraries in Britain and America in the late nineteenth century was linked to the democratic movement for public education. Before this concept became popular in the free public libraries, scholars and members of private, subscription, or student-society libraries were accustomed to open-shelf privileges in their own libraries. In German universities the "seminar method," in which books were presented in the classes where teaching took place, was widely used. This seminar method for advanced research and scholarship was adopted by the Johns Hopkins University (1876) and later by Harvard University.

As for academic libraries in general, Robinson (1876) advocated allowing the students free access to the books, at least for some hours during the weekend, on the ground that studying in the library was an important part of a student's education. Another reason was to expose students to books other than the ones they were directed to by instructors or by the catalog. This would help students acquire their own taste for books and encourage them to select and buy their own.

> A young man who spends four or seven years of student life where he can see a library, but cannot reach it, generally just fails of the only opportunity which is ever possible both to acquire the tastes and habits of a reader himself, and to prepare himself to mold the tastes and habits of others.
>
> (p. 517)

To broaden their knowledge and understanding of the subject they were studying and help them become self-reliant scholars, Robinson believed students should be encouraged to read more than textbooks. "To do this," however, "a man must stand face to face with the books required. An hour spent in turning over the books and making the choice is, perhaps, better than any two hours spent in the reading" (p. 518).

During the first quarter of the twentieth century over half the American academic libraries could be classified as "entirely or mainly open shelf" (Hyman, 1972). The academic collections continued to grow and became too large for convenient browsing. One of the ways used by universities to cope with the fact that the bulk of their collections was closed to students was the establishment of browsing rooms and browsing collections, containing books of a popular nature, selected and arranged for recreational reading. Usually these were circulated collections. Sometimes there were also books for courses, and also magazines and newspapers. Browsing rooms were located in the main library building or sometimes in the student union, and during the 1950s even in dormitories. The forerunners of these collections were several types of small private library available to students and faculty in the colonial colleges, where most of the collections were noncirculated. These included libraries in dormitories and student houses.

The closed stacks in academic libraries, on the one hand, and the increasing awareness at that time that the promotion of recreational reading was one of the functions of college libraries, on the other, contributed to the establishment of the browsing rooms, which were sometimes called "good reading collections." Browsing rooms grew both in number and in status during the 1930s and 1940s (Ellsworth, 1968; Marks, 1976). A survey carried out in the early 1940s revealed that 38 percent of American universities had "Browsing rooms" (Young, 1942). The average number of volumes in the browsing room was 3,000, with many of them (25 percent) also carrying periodicals. Of the universities which had browsing rooms, two-thirds noted that they were a great success. By the end of the decade the number of universities with browsing rooms had grown to 57 percent (Ricarda, 1949), while the average number of volumes they contained had risen to 3,500, with a third of them carrying periodicals.

Most large European libraries had closed stacks and preferred indirect bibliographic access. Following the example set by libraries in the United States, in 1894 James Duff Brown introduced open access in Clerkenwell Library in London. This was the first time that British library users were allowed direct access to the books on their lending library's shelves and hence the chance to browse (Goodall, 1989).

American ideas about libraries influenced the Diechman

Public Library in Oslo, whose librarian, Haakon Nyhuus, instituted open access to the shelves. This was seen by Fredrik Nilsson
of the Stockholm Workers' Library as "a bold decision" that
shifted "a considerable part of the work on the public" (Larsson,
1989, p. 11).

By the 1930s, direct access for browsing, along with shelf classification, had generally been adopted in both the United States
and the United Kingdom (Goodall, 1987). The provision of direct
access was part of a multifaceted political and socioeconomic
trend during the last half of the nineteenth century and the first
decades of the twentieth century. Some of the contributing factors
were: political democratization, urbanization, the spread of
public education, the growth of commerce and industry, migra-
tion and emigration (especially in the United States), and a rapid
proliferation of means of transport and communication.

By as late as 1950, Ranganathan addressed the issue and
argued with those librarians who

> propose to leave the trench, as it were, and to give up classifica-
> tion altogether, and to put their faith back in alphabetical
> arrangement . . . the débâcle appears to include even a serious
> proposal to revert to arrangement of reading materials in acces-
> sion order and to deny open access – the greatest human
> contributors of the library profession.
>
> (1951, p. 103)

After the Second World War, the academic libraries grew into
huge collections with millions of books. This resulted from the
upswing in book production, the spread of education and associated increase in the number of students, and the aspiration to
build comprehensive collections. The vast growth in the size of
collections made the problem of storage all the more acute.
Different solutions were attempted, among them the use of
microfiches and microfilms, which did not fulfill the hopes that
were attached to them.

There was a need, however, to find more economical and
compact storage systems. Systems that were proposed included,
on the one hand, storage by means of special technological
methods such as compactus (compact shelving) or automatic

storage, and on the other, storage of the collections or part of them in storerooms, i.e., closed-shelf storage. Closed-shelf storage enables economizing on the space between bookcases, as well as storage according to size for maximal utilization of the storage area. Since the public does not have access, it is possible to store books according to any criterion, such as accession number, book size, and the like. It is also possible to locate the storage room at a distance from the place where service is provided.

The growth of collections, then, forced the libraries to retreat, albeit partially, from the principle of direct access to the entire collection. In most of the large academic libraries nowadays only part of the collection is open to the public, including reference materials, new books, and books that have seen considerable use; whereas older books and less-used books (according to different criteria) are transferred back to the closed shelf.

Summary

In ancient times, when documents were set down on papyrus and clay tablets, their physical form dictated the closed-shelf storage system: i.e., crowded storage that was intended to preserve the documents. Access was limited to a restricted public.

In the Middle Ages, the use of books was even more restricted, and most of it was done in the monasteries. The books, of which there were few, were placed in cases. Sometimes books were loaned to people outside of the monastery, on adequate security, for purposes of study or copying.

With the rise of the university libraries, books were designated for on-the-spot use, and certain people were allowed direct access, especially students. To solve the problem of security and fear of thefts, books were fastened by chains to desks. Some of the university books that were designated for borrowing by students were kept in closed cases.

In the stall-library storage system and the hall-type system used in the fifteenth to seventeenth centuries, readers had direct access to the chained books. During the Renaissance and Baroque periods, the owners of libraries permitted use of their collections to a familiar public. With the eighteenth century, when both books and users of libraries proliferated, books began to be stored on multi-tier stacks and the public was provided with studying areas in alcoves that were added within libraries; again a separation was made between books and readers.

This tendency only gained momentum in the nineteenth century, when the spread of democracy brought the establishment of public libraries and public schools, the growth of universities, and the proliferation of educated people in society. Now there was a larger library public, much of which was no longer personally familiar to the librarians. Fears about the security of collections encouraged closed-shelf storage; only a limited portion of the books was placed in reading rooms for direct access.

Late in the nineteenth century, pioneering theorists called for free access to the bookshelves and for exposure of users to library materials. This began to be instituted in small library branches, in libraries for researchers only, in university seminary libraries, and in browsing rooms that were established for undergraduates. By the 1930s, free access to library collections was widely adopted in both the United States and the United Kingdom.

With the huge growth of the academic libraries since the 1950s and of public libraries since the 1960s, difficult problems of storage arose. Parts of collections began to be moved into economical storage on some floors of the library buildings or even into other buildings, sometimes even distant ones; precisely in a time of widespread education that emphasized independent study and investigation of sources, there was no direct access to a large part of the collections.

Will the technological epoch change this situation in the future?

5

The Accessibility of Materials

Provision of direct access to library materials still does not guarantee the full accessibility of these materials to the public, nor does an open-shelf policy eliminate the many obstacles on the way to the desired item or information. When direct access to library materials is available, ease of access to the materials is still dependent on a large number of factors (see below), some of which constitute barriers to the locating of items.

(a) Factors connected to physical aspects of the library and the organization of its materials. The influence of shelf arrangement on locating a particular item involves several aspects of the physical arrangement:

- The layout of the library
- The location of the desired bookcase in the library
- The location of the shelf (within the bookcase) on which the item is placed
- The ways the items are displayed

(b) Factors connected to library policy:
- Collection-building policy
- Decisions about specific acquisitions

(c) Factors connected to the method of stock management:
- Circulation
- Storage
- Misplacement

(d) Factors connected to the intellectual system of organizing the materials

Factors Connected to Physical Aspects of the Library and the Organization of its Materials

The layout of the library

A library's layout is a significant factor in the ease of use of both the building and the stacks, directly affecting the accessibility of the collection. While architects are very aware of the importance of the flow of people in a building, they are not always aware of the need for a structure that will facilitate the location of materials. The extremely large buildings of academic libraries that have been built since the end of the Second World War and the tremendous buildings of public libraries that were constructed in many cities during the 1990s have transformed the library into a huge and overwhelming structure, with large and imposing halls. Some libraries do have a relaxing and friendly atmosphere, but more often they strain the patron's orientation and are difficult to navigate successfully.

The complexity of public building design has been researched from several aspects, for example Weisman's (1981) study of ten University of Michigan buildings, which found a strong correlation between the reported frequency of disorientation in the buildings and the complexity of their floorplans, as rated by twenty independent judges. Best (1969) in a study of complexity of routes within a single building – a British town hall – found a number of variables to be associated with deviations from the direct route; the most powerful variable was route uncertainty. Route uncertainty was mentioned in several studies as contributing to the patron's general feeling of "lostness" in the library. This problem is usually solved by the provision of directional signs, which are a major component of a user-friendly library (Bosman and Rusinek, 1997). Simple floor plan and stack arrangements are recommended as well as clear and easily understandable signs providing directional and institutional information. However, one must be aware that over-zealous use of signs may lead to the unwanted effect of their being partially ignored.

In a study conducted in the library at Indiana University Northwest (IUN), it was found that although proper directional signs did help people to find their way around, they do not fully compensate for a complex floor plan (Bosman and Rusinek, 1997). David Kaser (1979), describing in his article the videotaping of the information-seeking behavior of graduate students in the library, showed the students misreading the signs and consequently making logical, but wrong turns.

Another component of way-finding is the user's knowledge of the library, which pertains to the patron's level of perceived familiarity with the library's spatial set up. In a study of 522 students from two public American universities, a correlation was found between the patron's sense of familiarity with the library and the number of library instruction courses undertaken and also with the relative frequency of library visits (Jiao and Onwuegbuzie, 1997).

In a study conducted in an American Southern university, the students were asked by their English instructors to maintain a diary of their search processes over a period. Of these students 75 percent to 85 percent (in each of the classes) described their initial response to the library as one of anxiety. They mentioned a feeling of "lostness" that stemmed from four factors (in order of influence): the size of the building, lack of knowledge as to where things were located, uncertainty about how to begin, and being unsure about what to do (Mellon, 1986).

A feeling of "lostness" pertains to the patron's spatial orientation within the library, and contains a psychological element. Bostick (1992) has coined the phrase "affective barriers" in describing feelings of inadequacy when using the library. Onwuegbuzie (1997), in his study of 81 graduate students who wrote a research proposal, reports students feeling uncomfortable or unsafe in the library. He uses the phrase "comfort with the library," i.e., how safe, welcoming or non-threatening the library appears in the eyes of its patrons. The feelings that are aroused by a building imply that buildings do "communicate", i.e., impart messages to the visitor:

> A library is a physical setting for many communications among users, librarians, and library materials. At the same time, users are affected, consciously or unconsciously, by messages coded in the building itself, in its architecture, decor, lighting, and furnishings, as well as in its signs.
>
> (Eaton, 1991, p. 519)

The location of the bookcase

The location and mode of presentation of the books on the shelf influence the user. The location of the bookcase within the library largely determines the accessibility of the items stored in it. Is the bookcase openly visible, close to central service points of the library (such as the reference desk, lending desks, reading corner, entrance, etc., or instead in a peripheral place or at the rear of the hall? The same considerations that are relevant to the location of stores in shopping centers and malls apply as well to the location of bookcases in the library space.

Goldhor (1972) examined the relationships between methods of book display and circulation. He compared two libraries; in one, a sample of 318 copies (102 titles) were put on display whereas in the other, almost the same books (234 copies, 105 titles) were shelved regularly. The displayed books were used more often than the regularly shelved books. Goldhor concluded that displays stimulate browsing and that browsing is a common way to locate fiction materials in public libraries.

In a second experiment by Goldhor (1981), in the area of adult individual biographies in a public library in Jamaica, similar results were found. Of a sample of 144 books, 66 books (55 titles) were placed on a prime display by the circulation desk, under the sign: "Good Books You May Have Missed"; 30 titles (39 books) were included in a book list of which 1,000 copies were distributed; and the remaining 39 books (30 titles) constituted the control group and were left on the regular shelves. A significant increase in circulation was found compared with the three-month pre-experimental period and with the control group. In the display group, the circulation increased seven times, and in the group of books on the list it increased four times compared with the pre-experimental period, with the number of loans of the books in the control group remaining essentially the same.

The location of the shelf on which the item is placed

An additional factor affecting the degree of exposure of the item to the potential user is the location of the shelf on which the item is placed within the bookcase.

Marketing experts recognize the importance of the height of the shelf on which a product is placed as a significant factor affecting sales. The various marketing agents maintain an ongoing struggle with the managers of department stores and supermarkets over the shelf on which a given product will be placed.

In a study by Cooper and Wolthausen (1977) at the Undergraduate Library of the University of California, Berkeley, a sample of ranges of shelves in the library was examined. The findings indicated that the higher the shelf, the higher the chance that its books will be used (the heights of the shelves were 16, 28, 40, 42, 64, and 72 inches from the floor, respectively).

Andrews (1988), in her study conducted at a public library in Florida, found that items on the third and fourth shelves (counting down from the top) were at eye level for most browsers and had the highest circulation statistics.

In other words, library users tend to choose and take books whose shelf height is convenient for them. It is not comfortable to stoop and kneel down in order to see what is on the low shelves of the bookcase. Thus, ease of access plays an important role in the process of selection of desired items by library users.

The way items are displayed

In regard to a shelf in a certain bookcase in a particular area of a library, there is still a question as to how the item has been placed on that shelf. Insofar as its placement will give it greater exposure to the quick glance of an information seeker, its chances of being extracted are greater. In business concerns that concentrate on sales one finds often special and even eccentric shelf arrangements, all of them intended to increase the chances that customers will notice them and take an interest in their contents. Managers of individual library collections who realize this have exploited this factor and arranged and placed the books and other library materials not in the traditional way, with their spines exposed to the space of the room, but "face-on."

At the Surrey County Library (England), as part of the policy of emphasizing the needs of the browsing reader, some proportion of the stock was placed face-front in order to stimulate interest and bring books to the readers' attention (Ainley and Totterdell, 1982). This same principle was employed in the Baltimore County Public Library by its director Charles Robinson and this arrangement contributed to an increase in circulation (*Give'em What They Want*, 1992).

In an experiment conducted by Sarah Long (1987) at a county library in North Carolina, a random sample of 50 books was divided into two groups. The test group books were placed face-front and the control group was displayed spine-out (all the books had a one-week circulation period). During the test period (two months), the average number of circulations per book for the control group was 2.58 compared with 4.7 for the experimental group. These results indicate the influence of face-front display on browsers.

Factors Connected to Library Policy

Collection-building policy

The dependence of browsability on librarians' policies and decisions is reflected in the selection policies of libraries. To begin with, not every library can build a comprehensive collection, even in particular subject areas, and as the building of collections becomes more and more selective readers need to use other search channels in addition to the local collection.

The collection-building policy reflects the conception of the library's purposes and is also affected by financial constraints. Although, in the past, American libraries tended to build comprehensive collections compared with the more selective approach of European libraries, since the 1970s, with the huge growth in book production together with budgetary difficulties, American libraries too have become more selective, on the assumption that inter-library loan can be used for unavailable titles.

In other words, those who formulate the selection policy of the library determine which material will be available on the shelves for browsers, as well as which subject areas will be more cultivated, which languages sought, and which kind of literature emphasized whether popular books or classic works, whether "trash literature" or "good books."

Thus, the composition of each collection reflects the selection policy of the library. Even if this policy is based on broad criteria, it will not always match the needs and desires of the individual searcher.

Decisions about acquisitions

In addition to the effects of the collection-building policy, the materials that the browser encounters on the shelves are also an outcome of decisions on acquisition or nonacquisition of individual items. The builders of the collection make individual decisions about whether or not to acquire each item, and these decisions can be subjective, arbitrary, and random. Decisions made daily by a team of librarians or by those entrusted to devise and approve the purchase lists determine the library's inventory to a large extent.

Factors Connected to the Method of Stock Management

Circulation

One of the problems that have been raised in regard to browsing among the shelves as a way to locate documents is the fact that most libraries are circulating libraries, which means that part of the collection, and in many cases precisely the newest, most popular, and most prominent books in their fields, have been borrowed and are outside the library instead of on the shelves. This common situation prevents the browser from exhausting the subject area in which he seeks material. The browser cannot be certain he has seen all the relevant materials owned by the library, nor can he recognize the full significance or richness of the collection's linear sequence if significant items are missing (Hyman, 1972, p. 203).

Storage

The size of libraries has made it necessary to deal with the problem of stocking. Among the means of coping with it are massive weeding, or the search for storage solutions, especially common among academic libraries. Storage entails keeping part of the collection in a separate place. Thus, in many academic libraries material considered less useful is kept in storerooms in the basement floor of the library building and material considered more useful is kept in reading rooms. This, however, compromises the principle of concentrating material on a certain subject in one place for purposes of browsing.

Here another factor enters in: the method, mode, and principles that determine what will remain in the central location of the collection that is available to the public and what will be removed for separate, secondary storage.

Sometimes stored materials are housed on regular shelving, placed according to a classification system, and users are able to browse the shelves. Sometimes it is not shelved by classification and instead is compact-shelved in a compactus. Sometimes the stored collection is held in a different building on the campus. On campus, open stacks are the most common type of facility used to store library collections (Cooper, 1991).

Storage sometimes also involves keeping part of the collection in storerooms in a different location altogether, off campus, but close by (usually a place where the land is cheaper) and near the freeway. In these storerooms, material is usually arranged not according to conceptual principles but according to various other criteria, such as size, which generally do not enable browsing.

In storerooms, economical storage systems are often used, such as placement of the books and documents according to their accession numbers, or placement on the shelves by chronological order or even by the physical size of the items. To achieve maximum economization in storage areas, sometimes technical strategies are employed such as the use of a compactus or even automatic storage; these do not allow access to the public.

Misplacement

As with libraries that offer direct access, the problem of misshelving (which also exists, on a smaller scale, in closed-shelf libraries) can lead to depletion and even great loss of books, harming the user's ability to locate material by means of browsing.

Cooper and Wolthausen (1977), who studied the issue of misplacement at the Moffit Undergraduate Library at the University of California, Berkeley, examined ranges of shelves looking for misplacements. Five and a half percent of the 9,818 books that were on the shelves that were examined were found to be misplaced; 66 percent of these misplaced books were misplaced on the shelves where they belonged, and the remaining 34 percent were misplaced on different shelves.

Factors Connected to the Intellectual System of Organizing the Materials

There is a relationship between the system of shelf and document arrangement and the activity of browsing. Many methods and tools have been systematically designed to permit or even encourage browsing. This applies to many information media, packages, and bibliographic tools as well as to the library itself. A book or a journal is usually organized to promote browsing. Such devices as the table of contents, indexes, introductions, and bibliographies both encourage and enhance browsing (Hildreth, 1982a). Particular information sources such as encyclopedias invite browsing by arranging topics systematically or by alphabetical order, and by supplying indexes, outlines, and section headings that help users quickly filter information (Marchionini, 1987).

Various forms of library catalogs, indexes, and abstracting publications or services, available in a manual or online format, incorporate features that permit browsing to one extent or another (Hildreth, 1982a). Many electronic information systems incorporate "browser" devices to enable easy use. The library itself is such a tool if its materials are stored and maintained in any other than a random manner.

The systematic arrangement of books on the shelves can be done according to different criteria: title, author, date, level of difficulty, and, of course, subject. With the latter criterion, books on like topics are arranged on the same shelves; i.e., arrangement by a classification system.

The main purpose of a classification system is to enable information seekers to browse through documents, or books on shelves (Svenonius, 1981; Losee, 1992). Classification systems in fact invite browsing. The question is whether such classification systems do place books on the same subject together. Especially in large libraries, even when books are placed close together, at the same time the system necessitates dispersal of many others. This fact is indeed the basis of every classification system. Each decision concerning the arrangement of facets of each class in the classification system determines which facets will be placed together, and also which facets will be dispersed. Moreover, different arrangements may well serve the interests of some groups of users better than others.

Losee (1992) asserted that a classification system facilitative of browsing should: assign classification values objectively; provide a single classification capable of classifying all possible documents; provide a linear structure; assign values to documents so that when one moves away from any document in either direction on a shelf or in a database, the documents become increasingly dissimilar.

Once an initial document has been located on a shelf in a library or in a window in a hypertext system, searchers often choose to examine related materials (Morse, 1970; Baker, 1986; Marchionini, 1987; Drabenstott et al., 1990). Losee (1993) examined the relationship between the shelf locations of books and the books users choose. He conducted a study of 96 randomly selected patrons and of all 577 books that they borrowed at the Davis Library of the University of North Carolina (Chapel Hill), focusing on the relationships between such factors as the distances between books taken out by the patron, the number of books chosen from each browsing area, and the number of browsing areas. Losee found that patrons typically borrow about three volumes at a time, and that roughly half of all patrons make more than one stop (the location to which a patron goes to begin browsing among adjacent and nearby similar books). Classification was shown to be beneficial by clustering together documents that patrons wish to circulate together.

The most common general classification systems are Library of Congress Classification (LCC) and Dewey Decimal Classification (DDC); Universal Decimal Classification (UDC) is prevalent mainly in technical and special libraries in Europe. The Library of Congress Classification system is suitable mainly for shelf arrangement and not as a retrieval tool. It is an enumerative system; its structure is sometimes illogical and often omits the hierarchical level. The notation is neither expressive nor hierarchical and consists of capital and small letters, numerals and decimal expansion; sometimes alphabetical subdivision is used.

Being highly detailed, the system enables focusing on very specific topics; on the other hand, not being fully hierarchical and logical, it does not offer a full representation of a subject. Usually, general books on a subject do not precede other books on that subject. Moreover, the alphabetical arrangement of subtopics means that the different subject areas are not reflected. Cochrane and Markey (1985) maintained that the Library of Congress Classification system is not a true classification system, since it has relatively little ability to demonstrate the relationship of one item to another.

The Dewey Decimal Classification system, on the other hand,

has a logical, hierarchical structure, and uses an expressive notation in decimal form. The clear hierarchical order of the different subject areas, and the use of decimal numbers to denote the subject and represent the position of the subtopic in the hierarchy, make available to the browser among shelves each subject within his field, with the broad subject area preceding it and the related subjects at hand, whether before or after, and easily identifiable.

At the same time, each of the systems, being based on the content of the books, provides a solution to the issue of the subject catalog. The DDC and the UDC use the same call numbers for classifying the books on the shelves and for preparation of the subject catalog; the Library of Congress, for its part, has developed two separate instruments based on different theoretical concepts, namely, the Library of Congress Classification System and the Library of Congress Subject Headings.

Since the late nineteenth and early twentieth century, librarians have had to deal with two different tools that focus on the content of the book, namely, the shelf classification and the subject catalog. This has raised the question of what each has to offer: do they cancel each other out, and which is preferable?

One of the first studies to address this issue was the dissertation by Kelley (1937), which compared classification numbers and subject catalog as retrieval tools. Kelley found that on average, three times as many titles on specific subjects could be traced under the subject heading in the dictionary catalog as could be found by direct consultation of the shelves. She concluded that searching for material on specific subjects by direct consultation of the books on the shelves is an unreliable procedure. She believed that the dictionary catalog could be made to compensate for the weaknesses of classification and to supplement its service to a considerable extent.

Ranganathan (1938), the founder of the Colon Classification, believed that the classification's class numbers are what leads the search to the specific subject, and not the catalog.

Bliss (1939), who developed the Bibliographic Classification System, agreed with him and believed that classification usually provides more satisfactory access to the books than does the subject catalog. "Classification is of especial service to research.

But it also facilitates access to particular books by placing them in smaller groups and consequently simplifying their arrangement and notation within the classes" (p. 158).

The editor of a study of patrons of five college libraries reported that 10 percent of the users of the subject catalog used it only to determine the most frequently assigned classification number under a heading, and preferred to make their selection directly from the shelves (Jackson, 1958).

Hyman (1971; 1972) collected opinion questionnaires from 152 librarians from 124 institutions in the United States and Canada. The results, which reflected what librarians thought patrons did, or expected them to do, revealed ambivalent attitudes about the role of classification in the direct shelf approach. Almost 60 percent considered shelf classification more important as a locational device than as a means of systematic subject approach; 58 percent agreed that subject headings in the catalog were more useful to the patron than shelf classification; only 43 percent thought the "average" patron could "follow" close classification notation on the shelves. Nevertheless, at least 65 percent of all respondents agreed on the desirability of open shelves – an opinion stronger among public librarians than among academic and special librarians. Most of the respondents regarded browsing as connected with "serendipity" and recreational reading, and denied its connection with open-shelf access and research.

Hancock (1987) concluded from her observation of 95 users (fully described in **chapter 6**) that subject searches were not initiated at the classified catalog. The great majority of searchers used the catalog or subject index to identify areas of shelves where they could pursue their subject search; individual titles from the author/title and classified catalogs seemed to be used merely to confirm the relevant subject areas.

Similarly, Hancock-Beaulieu (1990) concluded from her study of 200 users of the OPAC (On-line Public Access Catalog) in an academic library in London that the main subject-searching activity was undertaken at the shelves, and the bibliographic tools served to direct the searchers to the relevant areas of the collection. Searchers extracted a single class number that served merely as a location marker on the shelves. However, when at the shelves, classification played no part in narrowing or broadening a search.

The fact that a system that encourages browsing is used by patrons who have no clear idea of what they want or no specific titles in mind, exposes them to the influence of the shelf arrangement (Baker, 1986).

Browsing is indeed a widespread activity for locating materials in libraries. The popularity of this method is apparently attributable to its flexibility, and its yielding immediate results (unlike bibliographic searches that leave the library user, list in hand, to begin the search themselves). Browsing is also a pleasant activity: to weave through the shelves, find something, settle for a few minutes in an armchair or a corner of the library, look through the document and gain an impression, all adds up to a certain distinct experience.

The following chapters will discuss the information-seeking and finding aspects of browsing.

Summary

Direct access, which enables browsing among the shelves for locating scholarly and educational information in research libraries and for finding reading materials in public libraries, is dependent on a wide range of factors that determine ease of access. The provision to the public of access to a collection does not in itself ensure effective retrieval of the desired information.

To begin with, a browser relying on the local collection of a single library, is denied, even before the browsing activity has begun, any chance of locating certain items that simply are not in the library.

Moreover, certain physical aspects can hamper the browsing process – the structure of the building, its architectural planning, the clarity of the furniture arrangement, the lighting, the location of the bookcases, the crowdedness of the shelves, their height, and the ways the materials are placed. The size of the collection also affects the browsing process: the larger the collection, the more complicated and time-consuming the process is likely to be.

Along with these physical elements of the planning of the internal space of the library there are factors related to the use of collections: if the library is a lending library then some of the material, even if acquired and owned by the library, is not present on the shelves; especially if the material is up-to-date or popular, the chances are high that it will have been borrowed. Thus, at any given time part of the collection has been borrowed, and another part will have been misplaced.

And if all of these various factors were not sufficient, the system of arrangement of the material also affects browsing. The relevant question is: according to what principle have the documents been arranged on the shelves, since every system places certain documents together and disperses others?

And what of each searcher's level of skill at browsing and awareness of the potential of browsing as a tool?

Concepts of Browsing

The word "browsing" originally referred to animals' search for food, and particularly grazing. Jack London's *The Call of the Wild* (1903, p. 147) mentions "to browse the leaves of trees." The word was not associated with reading until the nineteenth century. Even modern dictionaries give the animal-behavior-related definitions first. In Webster's *Third New International Dictionary* (1961), "Browse" provides several reading-and-books-associated definitions: "to look over casually (as a book)"; "to skim through a book reading at random passages that catch the eye"; "to look over books (as in a store or a library) especially in order to decide what one wants to buy, borrow, or read"; "to make an examination without real knowledge or purpose."

LeBlanc (1995, p. 294) suggested that browsing the shelves or online catalog "is an activity that is not too far removed from the term's etymological origins in the sense that one draws nourishment from knowledge." Apted (1971, p. 228) cited an early use of the word "browsing" in the context of reading and books. James Russell Lowell, in *Among My Books* (1873), wrote: "we thus get a glimpse of him browsing for . . . he was always a random reader in his father's library."

In 1890, Professor James Hosmer of Washington University made what is probably the first reference to the browsing concept in the professional literature on librarianship (Hosmer, 1890). Hosmer attributed the practice of browsing to those who love books, whom he called "book-worms."

> Browsing is the proper Baconian method of reading. The rapture of having at command an entire alcove! As you pass along the

shelves, it is enough, in the case of most books, merely to touch the title page with the antennae; with others, a paragraph may here and there be tasted; as to few, content does not come until a chapter has been devoured; while for two or three, the conscience will not be appeased until they have been chewed and digested from cover to cover. Who can tell what books he wants without preliminary tasting? Titles often mislead, and never do more than hint at the contents.

(1890, p. 34)

This statement was made in a context where most libraries used the closed-shelf system; and Hosmer asked regretfully: "Could I not look along the shelves, try here and there, according to my nature; in a word browse, until I hit the exact bit?" (p. 36).

Browsing as a human activity has many connotations (Hildreth, 1982b); and as Hyman (1982) observed, it even has a touch of mystery. Morse (1973, p. 246) likened browsing to a search for targets in a war:

Browsing is a type of search, in many ways similar to the search, by an observer in a plane, for an enemy ship or submarine on the ocean surface. The observer is not sure the target is there, or that he will see it if it is there, but he flies a search pattern in the hope of success.

Morse described the browsing process as follows:

The eye does not move steadily along a shelf of books (or a line of print) absorbing steadily everything as it goes. It skips around, stopping a moment here, then jumping elsewhere. We pick up information in glimpses, as the eyes momentarily come to focus on a rather small area, subtending the fovea. Thus our perception comes to us in a sequence of glimpses, each glimpse conveying its pittance of information. In browsing we would spend a lot of glimpses.

(1973, pp. 246–7)

Browsing is one of the most common ways in which the library user finds the books he borrows. Morse (1970) suggested that the browser does not allocate his search effort at random; instead, he goes to that section of the library that he estimates has the highest probability of containing a book or books that his immediate interests would make him want to borrow. One can browse through a display of recent books to check new works, or through a portion of the library shelves in the hope of finding a relevant or interesting text; one can browse through the fiction collection to look for an attractive title; one can browse through the nonfiction collection to see whether any title seems interesting; one can browse through the periodicals and magazines for a new article; one can browse through the audio and video collections for something appealing; one can browse through the online lists of data banks; or one can browse or thumb through the card catalog (Morse, 1970).

Although the term "browsing" is widely used, there are different perceptions of what it means. Whereas Morse (1970) defined browsing as a search, Apted (1971, p. 228) described it as "an untidy operation – an activity which provokes new thought by exposing the user to a wide variety of stimuli, but without being planned to do so." Hildreth (1982b, p. 127) understood browsing as "a form of subject access to bibliographic information. Subject search may take the form of browsing among listings of materials to find items relevant to a topic or area of interest. In short, browsing is one means of ascertaining relevance."

Fussler and Simon (1969, p. 107) suggested a broader definition: "Browsing is the use of books that are not brought to readers by messenger." Ayris (1987) asserted that browsing should be viewed as a spectrum with a variety of meanings. He proposed three main variables that seem to influence the whole range of browsing activities:

(1) Definition of goal/aim.
(2) Nature of search strategy.
(3) Existing state of a reader's knowledge.

Some view browsing as only a supplementary technique (e.g., Bates, 1981; LeBlanc, 1995). Sometimes users come in search of known items, but also seek something more to supplement their expectations.

Hildreth (1982a, p. 184) disputed this view, arguing that for someone who engages in general browsing it "may be the primary technique employed, whether he is roaming the stacks or sitting at a terminal accessing an online catalog." Others consider browsing an essential part of the strategy of retrieval of material, whether the patron is looking for known items or is seeking library materials by subject (Atkinson, 1990). LeBlanc (1995) regarded "browsability" of library materials as an aspect of access that is provided by a consistent and predictable system of classification and that perhaps even has substantial value.

What do we gain from browsing? Shelf-browsing is a helpful bibliographic approach to library resources in all situations where it is not one specific title that is required, but one of a kind or a range of titles. Shelf-browsing is also helpful when a carefully selected group of frequently used materials is used primarily by experienced staff (in reference and bibliographic collections). It is also useful when the user knows the specific class number, including its limitations; and it can be useful for finding recently published materials (Boll, 1985).

Hildreth (1982a) observed that browsing is employed when the browsers' criteria of interest are not precisely defined and are subject to redefinition. People may wish to find previously undiscovered sources that accord with those uncertain criteria, whatever the publication format or "discipline of residence" of those sources turns out to be.

Bates (1989) suggested that the researcher browses because he is thereby exposed to a variety of related areas, some of which may be related in unexpected ways, thus producing serendipitous discoveries. Moreover, by browsing the researcher can look directly at the full text of the materials, and gain a quick, overall sense of the "feel" or character of an author and his approach. Such a sense is almost never accessible through any classification or subject description.

Marchionini (1987) asserted that people browse for three reasons:

(1) The search objective cannot be clearly defined. When looking for information people often proceed itera-

tively, beginning with a broad entry, browsing for documents related to that entry, and then browsing the documents for additional entry points. This approach to browsing is logical and systematic, and often yields satisfactory results.

(2) The cognitive burden of browsing is less than that of structured formalized searching. This may be because of cognitive laziness, or because browsing is a strategy that requires only limited, short-term memory for extraction and judgment of relevance; or it might reflect novice or casual users' poor understanding of how information is organized in a system.

(3) The information system supports and encourages browsing. For example, information sources such as encyclopedias invite browsing by providing indexes or outlines; a library's classification system invites browsing; users examine the card catalog to identify a subset of the collection; electronic, full-text systems offer opportunities to make a document available in many places simultaneously.

Herner (1970) made a similar observation:

Sometimes materials are arranged in such a way as to force or strongly encourage browsing; as with conventional new book and periodical displays, in which current materials are placed in prominent, readily accessible areas, to create maximum visibility for the users. Here we have a guided or externally induced browsing. In this regard the library resembles a supermarket, in which products that are being "pushed" are given particularly prominent position among the shelves.

(p. 411)

Gore (1973), in his *Bibliography for Beginners*, recommended the practice of "reading the shelves": "Any time you want to experience the joy of serendipity, go to the shelves and start browsing in some subject area that has caught your interest. This is called 'reading shelves,' an activity that is the hallmark of a mature reader." The simplest way to do this, he suggested, is: "When, by whatever means, you have located a book on the shelves that interests you, always take a look at the groups of books shelved to either side of it" (p. 76).

Fox and Palay (1980) described the process of browsing as a "heuristic search" in a well-connected space of records. Stone (1982) focused on the interactivity of the process and referred to browsing as "a means of serendipitous interaction with the materials of research." Marchionini, (1987, p. 69) made a similar observation: "Browsing is a highly interactive process with multiple decision points which depend on feedback to help determine what to do next."

Browsing, then, is not one but many things (Herner, 1970). There are different types of browsing; Celoria (1968) described four types:

(1) Higher browsing –where a user sets aside a regular time to survey library materials purely for the purpose of picking up any useful ideas.

(2) Chance discoveries – of, for example, neighboring words in a dictionary.

(3) General or utilitarian browsing – for example, looking at a row of periodicals out of interest (or need) to see what they are about.

(4) Purposive browsing – involving regular glances over current literature to keep up-to-date.

Herner (1970) distinguished between directed browsing and undirected browsing. Directed browsing occurs when a person starts out with a specific intent or goal, but does not know how to arrive at it. Thus, although the browser has a specific end in mind, he or she still goes through a browsing process. Undirected browsing occurs where there is no specific or conscious intent or goal. The browser merely "kills time," or sifts through a body of publications (in a news stand, in a bookstore, or in library shelves or the card catalog, for example) in the vague hope of finding something useful or interesting.

Probably the most common situation for the average person is something between directed and undirected browsing, as when a person habitually scans a given journal or newspaper. Most of the time this browsing follows a predictable pattern, starting with the table of contents of a journal, then turning to articles that appear to be of interest. The browser scans the front page of a newspaper, then turns to specific columns, then to the editorial, perhaps not knowing in advance exactly where information of interest is likely to crop up, but increasing the probability of payoff by choosing specific media (Herner, 1970).

Apted (1971) proposed a similar classification of browsing types:

- General browsing – purposeless browsing for pleasure.
- General purposive browsing – work- or study-oriented browsing; involves planned or unplanned examination of sources, including journals, books, or other media, in the hope of discovering unspecified new, but useful information.
- Specific browsing – browsing done by researchers and scholars; these users have some knowledge of the intended direction of their search, which is not casual or haphazard.

Hildreth (1982b) observed that browsing may be more or less planned and directed, or proceed casually through information sources from an initial information need or interest that is more or less well defined.

Buckland (1988) looked at browsing from only one standpoint and described it as an informal searching that is low on document specificity, but might at any level be of information specificity. He portrayed browsing as an essentially unsystematic activity that includes both vague searches for anything that might be of interest, and accidental and serendipitous situations in which highly specific information is found in an unsystematic way.

Baker (1986) also considered browsing an informal activity, but not necessarily an unsystematic one. He described a person in a public library who wants a new mystery title and goes to the new-book display to locate it. Once he is at the display, he may search among the 300 new mysteries to locate one that meets his desire to read an amateur-detective story.

Hancock (1987), after studying the search behavior of 98 users in a university library, defined two basic browsing activities when looking for library materials. The first was unstructured activity, whereby searchers (a) did not start at the beginning of the sequence of a given class number, (b) usually did not cover the entire class-number sequence, and (c) always backtracked in the immediate course of the search, progressing in a zigzag, irregular fashion, repeatedly going back over ground already covered. The second browsing activity was a structured one; here, the searchers progressed in a linear fashion to the end without any backtracking. Of the cases she studied, 77 percent were unstructured searches and only 23 percent were structured ones.

Marchionini (1987) suggested that there are many browsing techniques, ranging from random and informal to systematic and formal. These techniques depend on the object (information) sought, individual search characteristics, the purpose of the search, and the setting and context for conducting the search.

Goodall (1989) concluded from her literature survey that browsing can be described on three levels ranging from a haphazard and heuristic approach, to one relying on chance and common sense, to a systematic one. She suggested that whereas all three are employed at the academic library, in most parts of the public library only the first two techniques are used, with the third applicable only to the nonfiction collection. In that context, it is likely that more literate users browse with intent, either for known or for unknown items. Thus Goodall distinguished between scholarly browsing, which is particularly done in the academic library, and more general browsing, which tends to occur in the public library.

Beheshti (1992) portrayed browsing as an important and integral part of the information-seeking activities of library patrons. Browsing, in his view, falls into two broad categories: random and systematic. Random browsing is the nonpurposive, general type of browsing that tends to occur in public libraries and is mainly oriented to leisurely reading. Systematic browsing usually has the specific purpose of alleviating the user's information deficit. This type of browsing constitutes the first phase of more specific information seeking.

Mann (1994) maintained that the need for browsability is actually twofold. He described two kinds of browsing: "browsing proper," which allows users to gain an overview of materials on a given subject, a rundown of what is available; and "scanning," which is satisfied only by deep access and full text searching.

The study of browsing as a way of seeking materials has brought new terms into use, some of which serve as synonyms and some of which refer to different types of browsing. Some of these terms are surrounded by controversy. The literature contains such terms as: roaming; reading the shelves; scanning; serendipity. Hildreth (1982a, p. 181) spoke of "roaming among the shelf area of a library or bookstore to scan materials of potential interest." Gore (1973) called this behavior "reading the shelves." LeBlanc (1995, p. 295) used the word "scanning" as a variant verb to describe bibliographic "grazing" activities: "Pursuing systematically controlled headings in a catalog, scanning classified call numbers in an online catalog, or browsing classified texts on a shelf."

Bates (1989) mentioned "area scanning" as an information search strategy; it involves browsing the materials that are to be found near materials located earlier in a search. This technique is especially popular in catalog use, and is most commonly applied to books arranged by a library classification scheme on the shelves of a library. "With area scanning, one may either follow the exact arrangement of the classification scheme by reading linearly along the shelves, or alternatively, deliberately not follow the order," which she believed to be more common, and more useful (p. 416). "This technique represents a deliberate breaking up of the conventional classified order, while enabling the researcher to remain in the same general initial subject area" (p. 417). Area scanning is the quintessential form of browsing in manual environments.

Mann (1994), on the other hand, used the term "scanning" to describe deep access to full texts – that is, access to actual books and their entire contents rather than just to superficial, surrogate catalog records. "Depth of access is a function of the classification scheme's arrangement of subject related full texts next to each other on the bookshelves" (p. 12). According to Mann, scanning affords a very deep level of access to particular, highly specific bits of information that are too small to be noted on catalog surrogates, even by enhanced surrogate records with abstracts or tables of contents. "Scanning is not an open-ended searching, with no definite question in mind, in mere curiosity to see "what's available"; rather it has a very definite goal in mind – but the fact being sought is such that a precise source for it cannot be specified in advance, even after exhaustive computer searches" (p. 14).

"Serendipity" is another term used in the context of browsing. Mann (1994) used it in contrast to the term "predictability." Buckland (1988) referred to serendipitous situations, in which information was found in an unsystematic way. Hyman (1972) explained that the word was coined by Horace Walpole, and was based on the title of the Persian fairy tale "The Three Princes of Serendip," the heroes of which were always making discoveries, by accident, of things they were not in quest of. In *Webster's Dictionary* (1961, p. 2972), this word is defined as "an assumed gift for finding valuable or agreeable things not sought for." Today serendipity is sometimes used to mean browsing, and especially "accidental browsing" (Apted, 1971). Hyman (1972, p. 133) asserted that

> Neither on grammatical nor logical grounds does it seem correct to use the word as an apparent synonym for "browsability." First, because the word signifies a characteristic of the seeker rather than the collection; it is a personal "ability" or "gift." Secondly, the idea of "accidentally" finding valuable things one is not looking for is not relatable to any intellectual goal or activity.

Summary

The term "browsing" originally referred to animals' search for food, and became a concept referring to widespread behavior in the library domain. Browsing takes place in a bookstore; along the shelves of a library; among the catalog's cards or among the computerized catalog records; or within a reference book's or textbook's pages.

There are different browsing techniques along the spectrum from random, informal, and undirected browsing, where the searcher has no specific intent and thus progresses in a zigzag, irregular fashion, to systematic, formal, and directed browsing, where the searcher starts out with a specific intent and progresses in a linear fashion.

Some scholars view browsing as a crucial method of locating information and material when the search objective cannot be defined, or when structured, formalized searching is too time-consuming. Others regard browsing as only a supplementary search activity.

7

Browsing as an Information Retrieval Tool

Many scholars have sought to trace the paths, strategies, and techniques that are used in order to retrieve information. The interest in the subject of information-gathering behavior was encouraged by the series of tests carried out at the Cranfield Institute of Technology during the 1950s. Since then, a new discipline has developed that deals with information gathering. This wide field encompasses channels of access to information as well as the strategies and techniques employed by information seekers.

Ellis (1989) described information-retrieval behavior in a model that has six elements:

(1) *Starting* – activities characteristic of the initial search for information (a variety of ways of identifying references are used).

(2) *Chaining* – the following of chains of citations or other forms of referential connection between material (this includes both backward chaining, the identifying of references from a material, and forward chaining, the identifying of references to a material).

(3) *Browsing* – semidirected searching in an area of potential interest.

(4) *Differentiating* – the use of differences between sources as a filter of the nature and quality of the material examined.

(5) *Monitoring* – the maintaining of awareness of developments in a field through the monitoring of particular sources.

(6) *Extracting* – the systematic working through a particular source to identify material of interest.

Ellis considered browsing an important part of standard information searching.

Bates (1989) referred to information-use strategies as "berrypicking." Berrypicking involves the use of a wide variety of techniques, some of which are very standard whereas others entail a considerable amount of browsing. The strategies are:

(1) *Footnote chasing* (backward chaining) – following up of footnotes found in books and articles of interest.

(2) *Citation searching* (forward chaining) – where one begins with a citation, then finds out who cites it by looking it up in a citation index.

(3) *Journal run* – the identification of a central journal in an area, followed by location of the run of volumes of the journal.

(4) *Area scanning* – the browsing of the materials that are physically collocated with materials located earlier in a search.

(5) *Subject searches* – in bibliographies and in abstracting and indexing services.

(6) *Author searching* – the use of an author's name to check whether the author has done any other work on the same topic.

According to Bates (1989), area scanning is most commonly used with books arranged on the shelves of a library according to a classification scheme. Aspects of browsing for the purpose of locating reading materials have been studied by means of very varied research systems, including:

(a) Surveys – by means of interviews and questionnaires. Some researchers conducted interviews or distributed questionnaires among library users and scholars, with subjects being asked how they located the materials that they used. In some cases questionnaires were distributed when the books were borrowed; in others, at the time the books were returned. There were also, however, studies in which the questionnaires were attached to a sample of books in the library.

(b)   Tracking of the circulation of a sample of books.

(c)   Tracking of a sample of books by means of slips attached to the books, or marking of the books in order to monitor and ascertain which were used, and whether this was for study or for brief perusal, on the assumption that some of the use of reading materials is done in-house and is not expressed in recorded circulation transactions. Borrowing, indeed, constitutes only part of the use of library materials. It is clear, however, that the proportions between borrowing and in-house use are different in academic and in public libraries.

(d)   Observations – tracking of users, and their ways of locating materials, within the library.

The various systems of research indicate that browsing is an activity that, at least from a superficial perspective without looking more deeply into the interface among library users, is not very prominent, and moreover is not reflected in different kinds of documentation of library activity, though circulation functions are documented. One can also save search transactions done on the OPAC or in different databases. Additionally, the reference librarian will be aware of reference inquiries, even though they may not be formally recorded, because of the librarian's involvement in them. Searching by browsing, however, is most usually done by the users themselves, without consulting the librarian.

Voigt (1959) concluded from analyzing four different studies that one-third or slightly more of the sources of information were come upon and used without references to them in other sources; instead, they were found as part of a regular or irregular browsing through, and reading of, the most important journals in the immediate field of interest. Voigt found that the other means of locating printed information were: recommendations of colleagues – directly through meeting, or by distribution of reprints (10% to over 33%); the researcher's "built-in bibliography" and memory (6% to 20%); references found in books and in periodical articles (5% to 15%); published abstracts and indexes (4% to 7%); personal indexes and library card files.

Herner (1960) reported on a study of 181 users of the Library of Congress, in which the majority were looking for specific books and only a minority were browsers. He suggested that the main reason for going to the book stacks seemed to be dissatisfaction with the slowness and inefficiency of the book deliveries. Another cited reason was "to see what's on the shelves."

Bowen's (1961) two-month interview-study of 175 users of the University of Chicago Library revealed that only 5.3 percent of all materials used were found by "true browsing" methods, the rest by the card catalog and related means. The card catalog produced the more valued materials, whether these materials were checked out or not. As for the borrowed materials, more material was found through the catalog than through browsing.

Slater and Fisher (1969) analyzed 6,300 questionnaires in which respondents were asked what they were doing in the library: 24 percent said they were browsing or keeping up-to-date.

Greene (1977) examined 439 questionnaires filled in by a random sample of faculty who had borrowed books from the Georgia Institute of Technology Library. The subjects were asked how they learned of the books they had borrowed. Browsing was the most commonly used method of finding out about books (31.3%); then came references in a publication (26.2%); "from a library catalog" (23.9%); "from a colleague" (8.8%); "from memory" (5.1%); from some other source (3.7%). One percent of the respondents did not answer this question.

A different method of studying information-seeking behavior was employed by Harris (1977). Slips were placed inside 2,400 books from four different subject areas. These slips were not visible when a person was walking by a shelf; however, they had to be moved when the book was extracted. When checked, of the 2,400 books that had slips placed in them, 10.5 percent could not be found and were assumed to be on issue, 40.2 percent were found with slips undisturbed, and 49.3 percent were found with slips missing or disturbed. Harris concluded that a large percentage of the collection was receiving some consultation; the number was 20 times higher than the number of books being used at desks and not being reshelved. These findings indicate the central role of shelf browsing in library use.

Broadbent (1986) studied how 108 faculty members at a College of Humanities identified wanted items. The findings were: references in books or articles (23%); subject catalog (19.8%); printed bibliography (18.4%); browsing (17.8%); word of mouth (13.5%); CARS – Computer-Aided Reference, a service whereby a reference librarian searches online bibliographic databases for the patron (3.5%); and other (4%).

Knutson (1986) concluded from a study of 1,105 books in four subject areas done in a medium-size research library that many circulated books are found through browsing. Patrons used the catalog as a springboard to a shelf area where they could then go to browse for books or information needed. No significant association was found between the number of subject headings per catalog record and the books' circulation. He concluded, therefore, that browsing may play a larger role than does the catalog.

Fussler and Simon (1961; 1969) developed a questionnaire form that was attached to a sample of books in the stacks of the University of Chicago Library. The questionnaires were not visible unless the book was actually removed from the shelf. The sample included 841 titles, both monographs and serials, in physics and history. The authors concluded that books that received little recorded use also received little browsing, whereas books that received much recorded use also received much browsing, except for the highest-use books, for which extrinsic factors distorted the picture.

Fussler and Simon found that there was considerably more browsing (as measured by the number of touches) than recorded use for books housed in stacks that were open to a large segment of the reading population, with from three to nine times as much browsing as recorded use, depending on the regulations governing stack access and the nature of the subject. They recommended that for a very long period of time, if not permanently, the great majority of books in research libraries should remain accessible and only a small percentage, which have been infrequently used, should go to storage.

Fussler and Simon (1969) concluded that in libraries with open stacks, some portion of the use of books consists of browsing. They explained the fact that some books appeared to have more nonrecorded use in proportion to recorded use than others by two probable causes: (1) differences in circulation rules among libraries; and (2) differences in the relationship of recorded to nonrecorded use between one subject area and another, and between different kinds of materials, notably monographs compared with serials.

Hancock (1987) conducted an observation of a random sample of users of the City University Library (London) who were looking for books. The users were asked to carry on with their intended searching, and were observed. Out of the 95 cases, 27 strictly followed a specific-item approach, whereas 68 employed some subject searching in the process of the search, and almost all of these 68 ended up subject searching at the shelves. Of the 42 cases initiated as specific-item searches, 15, or about one-third, developed into subject searches.

Searchers who initiated a search for a known item employed one of the following search techniques: (1) if they failed to find the intended item, they looked for alternatives in the catalog or on the shelves; (2) having found the intended item, they looked for additional works; (3) they intentionally used a known item as a means of locating a relevant area of the shelves to carry out a subject search.

Over a period of seven years, Selth, Koller, and Briscoe (1992) studied both the circulation and the in-house use of 13,029 volumes (randomly chosen from a collection of 1.1 million volumes at the library of the University of California, Riverside), which contained monographs as well as serials in all subject areas. They concluded that many more books were examined in the library stacks than were circulated. Over the seven-year period, 11.2 percent of the monographs and 13 percent of the serials did not circulate but had some recorded in-library use; 19.5

percent of the monographs and 12.8 percent of the serials had no recorded in-library use but were circulated. Thus, 30.7 percent of the monographs and 25.8 percent of the serial volumes had some of one kind of use but not the other. Monographs received much more external circulation, serials more in-house use.

In a study conducted by this book's author in 1994–5 among scholars in two Israeli universities (some 477 questionnaires were collected, out of the 2,361 questionnaires that were sent to all faculty members of the two universities; a response rate of 20 percent), 464 replied to the question: Is it your practice to browse among the library shelves? Some 51.7 percent (240 scholars) said they browsed often; 37.9 percent (176 scholars) reported that they browsed from time to time; and 10.3 percent (48 scholars) answered that they did not browse. The responses point to a wide use of browsing among academics.

In a study (Wakeham, 1993) of how nurses look for information, 42 percent of the 251 participants reported using the library. The most common ways of finding information in the library were: asking the librarian, and browsing the shelves.

From his observation conducted at the University of New England library, New South Wales, Apted (1971) concluded that there are differences in browsing methods between disciplines, and certainly between scholars in the humanities, social sciences, and sciences. Natural scientists typically begin a literature search by using standard abstract indexes and guides. They also learn about sources from colleagues and from references in papers and books. Social scientists and humanists use these methods as well, but they also often search the literature itself. They are likely to engage in a purposeful search through files or newspapers and journals. They also tend to conduct a general reading in the field, in the hope of making a chance discovery of unknown or pertinent information or in order to acquire background information about the subject (Stevens, 1956). Therefore, social scientists and humanists must have freedom to range, more or less purposefully, through books in many fields and cannot be restricted to requesting the items they need by author and title.

Stone (1982) described the ways in which humanists work. To begin with, they work alone; the notion of the invisible college is less common here than among scientists. Secondly, humanists do not delegate literature searching; that is because the ability to delegate searching rests on two assumptions: (1) that what is required is known, and (2) that it can be communicated. Furthermore, humanists regard the search for information as an important task in itself. This may explain, in part, the notion of humanists' need to browse, which provides a means of serendipitous interaction with the research materials. Stone (1982) asserted that the humanist has a need to browse, real or imagined; and needs a wide range of materials; and to see original documents.

In the 1994–5 Israeli study (conducted by the author of this book), distinctive differences were found among the scholars with respect to the use of browsing as an information-retrieval tool. Browsing as a frequent method of material and information retrieval was employed by 59.5 percent of the humanities scholars compared with 49 percent of the social science scholars and only 42.9 percent of the science and engineering scholars. That is, the differentiation that was made by Stevens in the 1950s and by Apted in the 1970s was still valid in the latter half of the 1990s, despite the dramatic changes that have occurred in regard to reference tools, data banks, indexes, and computerized catalogs. For humanities scholars, study of the text itself, and independent searches, are still important, as they have been for hundreds of years.

In British studies very few references to browsing can be found before 1960; and in contrast to the American research, most British studies have been carried out in public libraries.

Luckham (1971) interviewed 1,685 users of two public library authorities (the central library and a branch in each authority) and 715 of these authorities' residents. His findings indicated that some borrowers' selections were very purposive and direct; these users went straight to particular shelves or sections. On the other hand, among some users he found a more leisurely process whereby borrowers walked among various shelves, taking a book almost at random, and even after browsing through various books appeared uncertain as to which to borrow. Sometimes, when they were unable to find a suitable volume, they turned to the returned-book shelves.

Goldhor (1972) reported on an experiment he conducted in two Illinois public libraries, where 110 "good" books, half of them novels and half nonfiction, were chosen. The circulation of these books in the two libraries was tracked over six months. Then, in one library (the experimental library), 318 copies of 102 titles (out of the 110) were shelved on a book display in the reading area. In the second library (the control library), 234 copies of 105 titles (out of the 110) were left on the standard library shelves. The circulation of these books was then tracked for an additional six months. In addition, half of these books' borrowers were interviewed by telephone or by mailed questionnaires.

Goldhor found that in the experimental library there was an increase in the use of these books, whereas in the control library, use of the novels decreased and use of the nonfiction stayed almost the same. Goldhor concluded that adults borrow books from the public library as a result of browsing and that facilitating browsing will significantly increase circulation.

Marsterson (1974) concluded from his survey of the public library in Maltby that 38 percent of the books were selected by browsing. Spiller (1980) investigated the pattern of browsing of 500 borrowers in four British library systems, at the time when they returned novels, and also examined 1,314 novels which they returned. He found that 46 percent of the titles had been chosen exclusively through browsing. He suggested that browsing is used when the patron does not know the literature or cannot remember the author's name, but also is an expression of the freedom to choose, a rejection of the critical establishment, and an affirmation of confidence in the borrower's own critical judgment.

Spenceley (1980) interviewed 100 public library users in Sheffield, England, when they were leaving the library or returning books: 46 percent of the books were chosen because of the author; 13 percent because the author and title were known; 4 percent were previously reserved; and 37 percent were chosen simply because they "looked interesting on the shelf."

Ainley and Totterdell (1982) found that some 55 percent of the users in central and district public libraries, and 75 percent to 80 percent of the users in smaller branch libraries, are browsers.

An interview survey of a random sample of 226 local public library users in Australia revealed that 48.2 percent of them came to the library to choose materials by means of browsing; only 16.4 percent came to the library for specific information; and another 18.1 percent came to obtain a specific item (Willard and Teece, 1983).

In an examination of 198 books, randomly chosen from the adult collection of a small public library in Monticello, Illinois, the circulation for each title over a 14-week period was ascertained (Aguilar, 1984). The catalog cards of a portion of these books were withdrawn from the card catalog. It was found that the removal of the cards had no statistically significant effect on circulation. In addition, questionnaires were given to patrons who borrowed from the research-sample books. It was found that most of them did not have specific titles in mind when approaching the library, and that most did not use the card catalog, whereas browsing had a major influence on the selection process.

Harrison (1984) interviewed 200 people in two public libraries in Nottinghamshire, England. She found that most who looked for fiction books used a combination of browsing and searching for authors: 57 percent were mainly or exclusively browsers.

Jennings and Sear (1986) interviewed 135 borrowers as they left the public library. Of the books they were borrowing at the time, 34 percent were chosen by browsing; 61 percent of the borrowers said they had browsed and then recognized the name of the author. Browsing was also the main way these readers discovered new authors.

Turner (1987) employed a different method. A sample of 150 recently published literary-fiction works were tagged, and each was given a sticker inscribed "please insert questionnaire." Whenever these books were borrowed, the staff at the issue desk would insert a questionnaire and when the books were returned, the staff collected the completed questionnaires. The study was conducted over six weeks; 115 questionnaires were collected. It was found that 80 percent of the books were located while browsing, as the book caught the borrower's eye; 14 percent of the books were chosen by a combination of browsing and previous knowledge about the book.

Goodall (1988) found from interviewing 1,681 people in four public libraries that just over one-fifth of them found books, both fiction and nonfiction, by browsing. Goodall (1989) interviewed 200 users of a public library in Nottinghamshire. This library was designed to be "browser-friendly." Nine out of ten users chose their books by browsing; 23 percent recognized the author or title while browsing; 66 percent browsed and then chose a book that looked interesting. The interviewees were asked to indicate from which types of shelf they had borrowed books. The A–Z shelves were used the most, followed by the shelves of returned books, the spinners (popular paperbacks), the categorized shelves (romance, mysteries, science fiction, Westerns), and the displays (fiction books on a theme).

Research in information-gathering behavior in public libraries has focused almost exclusively on patterns of choosing material to be borrowed from the library. This fact may be attributed to one or more of several causes:

(a)   one of the major functions of a public library is its lending facility;
(b)   the most popular of public library services is the lending facility;
(c)   statistics on the lending activities of public libraries are easily gathered.

In contrast, the present author has conducted research on information-gathering behavior in the reading room (reference collection) of the public library.

The present study was conducted on a representative sample of public libraries in Israel during the years 1996–8, in the course of which 512 questionnaires were collected. These were handed out to people (grownups and young adults) who were present in the reading room and using its materials. The respondents were asked how they found out about materials they were currently using. The answers received (490 in number) were as in table 7.1.

Table 7.1 Sources of information on reading room materials

From teacher/lecturer/course bibliography	165	33.7%
Recommended by a friend	36	7.3%
Stack browsing	145	29.6%
From the library catalog	27	5.5%
Recommended by librarians	86	17.6%
Other	31	6.3%
	n = 490	

This research indicates that browsing by the user in reading-room stacks is also an important means of finding material (29.6% of searches). It is second only to recommendations from a teacher/lecturer or a course-work bibliographical list (33.7% of searches).

Atkinson (1990) found browsing to be the method most often used to learn about printed information sources, and suggested that it is an essential part of the strategy for retrieval of material. This, he maintained, is true whether the patron is looking for known items or is seeking library materials by subject; browsing is the primary retrieval system for a very large portion of library searches.

Some studies have focused on the characteristics of the browsing process. Morse (1970) suggested a formula to measure the chances of spotting books as a function of the ratio of search effort. The browser glances along the shelves of some section of the library for a length of time. Thus, the information conveyed to the browser comes in a series of glimpses. Morse regarded 1,000–2,000 books as an effective size for a section on a particular subject, that could be covered in a half-hour. If the section became larger, he recommended splitting it into a section of less often used books and a high-use section for browsing.

In her study of 515 patrons of the physics library at the University of California, Davis, Ross (1983) found that the mean time the patrons spent at the shelf was 9.4 minutes. One-third of the browsing activity took three minutes or less, and 20 percent lasted for at least 15 minutes.

Bowen (1961) found in her one-day survey of 183 users of the

University of Chicago Library that on average, 5.4 books were looked for in 33.8 minutes, that is, 6.2 minutes per book per patron. Faculty looked at more books but spent less time with each.

Hancock's (1987) results were similar to Bowen's. She found that on average, searchers examined six items on the shelves and selected two out of the six for further consultation. Ross (1983) likewise found that half of patrons removed two books or less; nearly 25 percent inspected five or more books, and about 4 percent looked at ten or more.

Browsing the shelves was found to be an unstructured activity in 77 percent of cases (Hancock, 1987). Most searchers did not start at the beginning of the sequence of a given class number; nor, for the most part, did they cover the entire class-number sequence, instead progressing in zigzag, irregular fashion. Only 23 percent of the observed library patrons started at the beginning of the class sequence and progressed in linear fashion to the end.

Searchers came to the shelves with one class number in mind and tended to browse only within a single class number regardless of whether they took a different shelf approach or first consulted a bibliographic tool. Only 24 out of 69 cases browsed beyond a given class number, following a negative (14 cases) or positive (10 cases) initial result at the shelves. Once the searcher had reached the shelves, the class numbers themselves seemed to have a negligible influence on furthering a search, the main criterion being the titles on the spines of the books.

The studies on browsing have generally not distinguished different levels of browsing. Most have related to it as a single mode of information seeking. The only study that has looked more deeply into the different kinds of browsing is the one done by Fussler and Simon at the University of Chicago Library.

Fussler and Simon (1961; 1969) attempted to evaluate levels of value for browsing. Browsing was considered "not valuable" if the patron merely glanced at the title page or only skimmed through the book while standing up ("loose-core" use). A higher level of browsing was "tight-core" browsing, consisting of: (1) checking the book out of the library; (2) carrying the book to the desk to read it there; (3) noting the title for future reference; or (4) examining a specific passage in the volume.

Effectiveness of Browsing

Many claims have been made over the years about the drawbacks and limitations of browsing. Some scholars have regarded browsing as a random search activity that achieves only random results; for instance, Urquart (1976) takes an extreme view and asks:

> is it [browsing] really a sensible activity in a research library? Does not the research worker really need whatever is published in the world which may be of interest to him rather than what he accidentally stumbles across in browsing around the shelves? Is the browsing habit but the survival of an accident custom or does it survive owing to bibliographical laziness or ignorance?

Gordon (1969), acting director of libraries at the University of Kentucky (Lexington), raised the issue of what advantage actually lies in browsing in light of the dogma accepted in the profession that it is the librarian's duty to "get the right book to the right person at the right time." Gordon suggested that with the removal of the barriers between books and readers, this concept has gradually changed to "let the user go to the collection and find the book he thinks will best suit his needs."

Thus Gordon inquired: "Is it really in the best interest of the reader to turn him loose in the collections to seek his own salvation? Will he find the right book?" (p. 1844). Here the library user's ability to exhaust the possibilities of browsing and find the right book, without help and guidance, is placed in doubt. Indeed, in Gordon's view "our current practice of intermingling books and readers and easy access tends to discourage, rather than encourage library users from seeking guidance in using the library" (p. 1845).

Similar doubts were raised by Wood (1977), who questioned whether users have enough knowledge about browsing, and suspected that the recourse to browsing stems from users' lack of awareness of the guides to the literature, so that they use the shelves as a replacement. The question is whether this replacement is effective.

LeBlanc (1995, p. 295) represented this approach with her assertion that the maximum value of browsing cannot be ensured without some mediation by the library staff. She claimed that the value of serendipitous discoveries can only be fully realized by the introduction of a predictable, systematic arrangement of materials on the shelf or in a catalog.

Morse (1970), on the basis of his assumption that the information conveyed to the browser comes in a series of glimpses, sought to develop calculations for how a library might be arranged to aid the average browser. He concluded that the librarian should arrange the collections so as to be obviously differentiable, in terms of interest potential, to the majority of library users.

A library that enables quick selection of a relatively few, small sections of high interest potential is the library that is most efficient for browsers to use. To help browsers, Morse (1970) suggested arranging the books on the shelves by subject. When the collection grows and becomes too large for all of it to be easily available to all users, and when even one class becomes too large for the generalist browser to cover effectively, Morse advised possibly dividing the collection into a low-use section to be stored separately and a high-use section for browsing. He believed the division should be based on circulation rate.

Although proponents of browsing have assumed that the large collections that characterize academic and research libraries as well as large public libraries enable the user to make interesting discoveries, it has become clear that very large collections are actually very time-consuming for the user since it takes longer to search the shelves. Thus, Rovelstad (1976) asserted that by means of browsing, the researcher can access only a small portion of the library's potential information resources with a great expenditure of time. The larger the collection, the greater the dispersal of subtopics. Oddy (1977, p. 2) notes that "In a large library, books which are potentially useful to one reader may be widely separated spatially."

There is apparently a maximum size for an open-shelf collection beyond which open shelves become a liability and even a disservice to readers and staff. Boll (1985) suggested that 1.5 million volumes, including bound serials, is the cutoff point.

Baker (1986), in addressing the issue of coping with large collections, made the related observation that "users browsing for a good book to read can easily be overloaded by the large number of possible choices, and may, therefore, adopt simplification strategies to limit their selection."

Despite the fact that browsing is a major means of locating information, few studies have tested its effectiveness. Fussler and Simon (1961) found that 56 percent of a sample of physics and history volumes removed from the shelves by users were located by browsing. Of these browsers, 46 reported that they had made some use of the books discovered in this way.

Greene (1977) examined the relationship between the channel by which a book was discovered and its subsequent value to its user. He studied a sample of 431 faculty users of the Georgia Institute of Technology Library and found (p. 316) the information given in table 7.2.

Table 7.2 Means of discovery and usefulness of books

How the book was discovered	Essential usefulness
Memory	42.9%
Reference in publication	40.7%
From a colleague	39.5%
From the library catalog	26.5%
Browsing in the library	18.3%

Here, browsing yielded the poorest results of all the search techniques. Only 18.3 percent of the material discovered by browsing was classified as "very useful," compared with over 40 percent of the material found by reliance on the searcher's memory (i.e., the searcher's awareness of the item), or by means of a reference in a publication. Location by means of information from a colleague (39.5%) or by use of the catalog (26.5%) also gave better results.

Browsing, then, ranked last among all the methods of locating books when the usefulness of the books discovered was considered. Greene concluded that browsing is the least effective way of locating books.

Slater and Fisher (1969) examined 6,300 users of British technical libraries. The average number of documents consulted was 4.1, and the average number of these that were found useful was 2.1; 57 percent of the users considered their visit to the library a success, and another 24 percent thought their visit a partial success.

In a study of 100 patrons in a public library in Sheffield (England), it was found that of patrons who had chosen books on the basis of prior knowledge of the author, 67 percent were pleased with their choice. Only 40 percent of patrons who had chosen books through simple browsing were pleased with their choice after reading the book (Spencely, 1980).

Goodall (1989) reported on a survey of 463 books that were returned to a public library. When the author was familiar to the reader, over three-fourths of the books had been enjoyed. When books were chosen without regard to the author, not quite two-thirds of them had been enjoyed. If the author was unknown, readers were twice as likely not to finish the books.

Jennings and Sear (1986) reported that 80 percent of users who had purposively chosen the books they had borrowed (especially books by specific authors) said they enjoyed the books, compared with only 35.56 percent of those who had browsed and felt that a book looked interesting. Of these, 21 percent did not finish reading the book, compared with only 3.85 percent in the previous category.

Summary

Browsing the library shelves is one of the main ways of locating material. In public libraries browsing plays a central role, especially in finding reading material for free reading. A small percentage (only 15 percent to 18 percent, Baltimore County, 1992) of public library patrons use such search means as catalogs. The large majority of public library patrons, over 60 percent, go to shelves of different sections of the library in order to find reading material of interest to them.

Users of public libraries' reading rooms (reference collections) also search for material by browsing in the open stacks, but to a lesser degree – 29.6 percent of the searches.

Especially interesting is the fact that today, in research libraries as well, browsing constitutes an important mode of location of materials, and researchers commonly wander among the shelves for purposes of information search – despite the computerized catalogs, online bibliographical databases (some of which are also available on CD ROMS), and other sophisticated search systems.

Although studies done over the years report different percentages, one may state that over one-third of researchers use browsing as a way to search for and locate information. This fact contradicts predictions about the abandoning of the library and transition to using sources that today are already available from the researchers' office, and which could save them the trouble of leaving the office and going to the library building.

Significant differences were found among scholars from the different faculties. Humanities scholars perform more browsing than social science scholars, and the latter perform more browsing than science and engineering scholars. The much greater reliance on browsing by humanities scholars stems from the fact that they are more interested in general reading in the field, as well as in background reading on their topics of research and other related topics; that they do less delegation of literature searches, instead regarding the search itself as part of the research process; and that they consider the search for documents as an important part of their work, and value having direct contact with these documents. In other words, the texts themselves still constitute the "research laboratory" for humanities scholars.

At the same time, it has emerged from individual studies that this search method yields fewer useful or enjoyable books than other modes of information retrieval. This points to a need for further studies to assess the value of browsing. However, this finding at least gives an indication about the limitations of browsability.

The question that arises is whether the transition to digital texts will eventually also change work habits and the means of location of information and materials of the humanities scholars, as it will certainly change these for the natural science scholars, for whom the most important instrument is the laboratory, and the text is only a secondary tool.

8

The Conjunction of Readers and Documents

This book has dealt with the various factors affecting the conjunction of document and user, book and reader. This conjunction is facilitated by three central factors:

- The documentation, storage and preservation of information
- Physical access to documents
- Formal and informal channels of information brokerage (for example, the formal surrogating of documents for bibliographic control and informal browsing), for bringing the documents to the notice of the user.

Documentation

The encounter between the reader and the document has existed since antiquity. It was made possible by a succession of technologies that began very long ago with the invention of writing, which enabled the transmission of information not only orally, as previously, but also by means of inscription and documentation.

The invention of writing made documentation possible. Additional technologies were required: the writing surface and the writing implements. Over the centuries different formats were developed for information storage, reflecting the technologies of the time. The creation and production of documents required that they be stored, and thus archives and libraries were established in which documents were maintained and registered. The structure of the archive or library, as well as its internal arrangement including baskets, shelves, and storage closets, also reflected the technologies of the time.

Accessibility

The determination of who would have access to stored documents reflected the characteristics of a society at the time, as well as of technology. In antiquity, libraries were designated for a very small group of people in the ruling class. In the ancient Near East, a scribal culture prevailed; literacy was restricted to a small, special social group. Even many of the kings were completely illiterate. In Greek and Roman times, wealthy people established private libraries; the possession of such a library was a matter of prestige.

In the early Middle Ages in Europe as well, there was a sort of scribal culture. Literacy declined, and the copying and study of books were the province of monasteries. Even there, the Church Fathers did not permit direct access to all of the books; books which they thought might have an undesirable influence were withheld from the monks. The monasteries lent books only to special, very distinguished individuals (in return for a considerable monetary deposit); most lending was to other monasteries for purposes of copying.

With the development of the universities in the thirteenth and fourteenth centuries, basic books were lent to students, but most of the collection was kept on closed shelves. During the thirteenth century, however, a change occurred in the encounter between readers and books. Part of the collection was fastened with chains to the shelves and tables, and readers were permitted direct access to these books.

This practice of fastening books with chains was widespread for a few hundred years, and ended in the eighteenth century with the growth in the size of collections; it became common practice to store most of the collection in a separate room or rooms, except for a few reference books that were placed in the reading room. This was also the approach in the nineteenth century, during which readers proliferated, most of them not personally familiar to the librarians.

The accessibility of documents was also affected by the technologies of each period. So long as the production of documents was complicated and expensive, accessibility was limited. When technologies enabled cheaper production, documents became accessible to wider publics.

It is possible that in the future, computer technology will enable full, direct access to documents such as the wide public has not enjoyed so far. Today, there are still constraints that prevent access for many. Exposure of digital documents requires the possession of a computer or access to a computer, in the workplace or in libraries. Large parts of the public in the industrialized states, let alone in the rest of the world, still lack direct access to computers and to computer communication.

Channels of Mediation

For the encounter between reader and document to occur, channels of mediation, such as bibliographic tools, are required. The traditional bibliographic tool was the inventory, which reflected what was available in the library and listed the items according to their arrangement on the shelves. In antiquity, inventories were displayed on the walls of the rooms in which documents were stored, and on clay tablets.

One of the oldest lists of books is a Sumerian tablet found at Nippur, and dated to 2000 BC, on which 62 titles were recorded. On the walls of the temple of Edfu in Egypt, names of books were found carved. Inventories constituted the first versions of catalogs of collections. The word "catalog" comes from the Greek phrase "*kata logos.*" *Kata* means "by" or "according to," and *logos* means "reason" (Strout, 1956).

A famous Greek catalog is the "*pinakes*", compiled by Callimachus at the Alexandrian library in the third century BC. These *pinakes* are believed to be a library catalog or a bibliography of Greek literature. The list contains the number of lines in each work, the opening words, and some bibliographic data on the authors.

The *pinakes* were arranged according to broad subjects; and within those, according to authors. This arrangement reflects the Greeks' attitude toward the author, which stemmed from the importance attributed to the individual person in Greek culture. Strout (1956) explains the emergence of catalogs as resulting from an "encyclopedic period rather than a creative period. It was a time of gathering, compiling and organizing the works of previous generations." It was natural, therefore, that in this period catalogs were created along with anthologies, dictionaries, and collections of excerpts.

In the Middle Ages, catalogs were created in the monasteries. One of the earliest listings of the holdings of a medieval library dates from the eighth century. It was written on the last flyleaf of a book and consists of a list of brief titles with authors appended to a few of them (Strout, 1956). The arrangement follows no order; it may have represented the shelf arrangement, done according to acquisition or size. In those days, it was common to bind a few works together and to list only the first work in the inventory lists.

The library at Reichenau, Germany, compiled several catalogs between 822 and 842. One of these included an enumeration of gifts; another listed the more valuable books. Only the first catalog maintained an order, mostly by subject and then by author. These catalogs referred to all of the works in each volume, which was quite exceptional in that period. Another exceptional catalog is that of the Benedictine house of Saint Trequier, 831. It used author entries, although in no order, and referred to all of the works that were bound together in each volume (Strout, 1956). These two catalogs were advanced for their time; though for hundreds of years, short inventories accompanying collections of books were prevalent.

In the late thirteenth century a union catalog was constructed, which included a unified list of holdings of English monastery libraries, "Registrum librorum Angliae," in which each library was assigned a number for coding purposes.

Only later did the catalog become a *finding list*. The catalog of Saint Martin's Priory (1389) was divided into three parts. The first was a listing by call number. This included, for each entry: a short title, the number of pages, and the number of works contained in the volume. The second part, also arranged by call number, gave the contents of each volume. The third consisted of a catalog of analytical entries and an alphabetical listing, once by author and once by title (Clark, 1902; Strout, 1956). This analytical catalog constituted an attempt to aid in locating material, and marks the beginnings of conceiving of the catalog as a finding list.

In the fifteenth century the use of cross-references appears; it seems initially to have been intended to serve the purpose of analytical entries. Toward the end of the fifteenth century, the German bibliographer Johann Tritheim added an alphabetical author index to a bibliography that he compiled in chronological order. In addition, the classified catalog of Syon Monastery, Isleworth, England, in the first half of the sixteenth century, included an alphabetical author index.

The addition of authors' names to catalogs listed by broad subject categories (corresponding to the way the books were placed on the shelves) apparently stemmed from the difficulty of locating material, as categories proliferated. In the introduction to the catalog of Feuillants de la rue Saint-Honoré (1765), it is argued that the arrangement of books by subjects involves great difficulty and makes errors likely. Therefore, it was decided to attach to the last volume of the catalog a detailed list by authors' names (Franklin, 1867).

The seventeenth century saw a strengthening of the concept that the catalog should serve as a finding list. Gabriel Naudé ([1627], 1950) stressed the importance of the catalog as a means of finding books. The catalog of the Bodleian Library of Oxford University (1620) was arranged by authors' surnames regardless of where the books were shelved. The listing of books by author's name constituted an author-ordered finding list of books (Ranz, 1964; Frost, 1976).

The French Code of 1791, which is the first national cataloging code, deals with each particular book, which provides the information for the entry (Verona, 1959). The emphasis on the book rather than the work manifests the then prevalent concept of the finding list.

In colonial America, many catalogs were arranged by the size of the books and sometimes by the names of the donors of books. The 1723 catalog of Harvard College was arranged first by size and then alphabetically by the first letter of the entry word.

Only in the first half of the nineteenth century, did the need to assist the reader in using the library lead to the building of indexes to the library collections. This sometimes also took the form of supplemental biographical notes on the authors in the catalog – for example, the Brown University catalog arranged by Jewett; and was extended by Edward Johnson, who added to the catalog that he arranged for the New York Mercantile Library many of the subject-grouping paragraphs that called attention to books not presented in the collection but judged of importance.

In the nineteenth century there began a slow transformation of the catalog, from serving as a finding list toward becoming a *collocating device*. Panizzi's 91 rules (British Museum, 1841) transformed the catalog, to some extent, into a collocating device, by detailing some of the uses of cross-reference. There are references, for example, from different forms of authors' names. The change in the concept was manifested in the work of Charles Ami Cutter (1904), who was the first cataloger to develop a theory on the purposes of the catalog. He specified three main "objects" of the catalog:

(1) To enable a person to find a book of which either
(a) the author, (b) the title, or (c) the subject is known.
(2) To show what the library has:
(d) by a given author, (e) on a given subject, or (f) in a given kind of literature.
(3) To assist in the choice of a book:
(g) as to its edition, or (h) as to its character.

This was the prevalent approach in libraries and in cataloging codes until the mid-1960s.

Project MARC, which was conducted at the Library of Congress in the mid-1960s, opened the path to the construction of computerized catalogs and the development of catalogs that are essentially sophisticated tools of retrieval.

The rules of cataloging as expressed in the catalog codes did not reflect the change immediately, but in practice the computerized catalog made possible more numerous points of access, as well as referrals from different forms of listing of names or subjects. Thus it enabled, to begin with, the full realization of Cutter's second "object": to show what the library has by a given author, on a given subject.

In addition, the computer now created, with the development of more sophisticated software for cataloging, additional possibilities of retrieval. The great breakthrough was the ability to search words within a record's field, which eliminates the former dependence on the order of listing of the words that constitute the field. This also adds possibilities of: Boolean search capability (a search that allows for the combination of two or more keywords); the capacity for truncation; the capacity for limiting the search to certain fields or a group of fields; the filtering of retrieval by date, language, medium, and so on; and the possibility of weighting the indexing of the document so that the retrieval will be relative to the searcher's request.

The nature of the catalogs, as well, stemmed to a large extent from the current technologies. Technology was what dictated the physical format of the catalog. And the format, together with the practical and economic difficulty of producing it, to a large extent dictated the theoretical principles of the catalog's organization. The book catalog makes updating difficult, since the preparation of such catalogs is complex and expensive; yet they reflect the situation at a given time, and much time passes until the preparation of a new catalog. Oxford University issued its first catalog in 1605, the second in 1620, and the third in 1674. The University of Leiden brought out its first catalog in 1595, and the second 45 years later in 1640. These huge gaps of time indicate the economic difficulty that was entailed by the printing technology, which prevented more frequent publication of catalogs.

The catalogs were single-entry catalogs; this also reflected the constraints of the technology, which until the late nineteenth century made the production of book catalogs costly. As a result, an entire concept developed in the area of cataloging that focused on the main entry. Indeed, if technological constraints dictate only one listing of each record, there is a need for a decision concerning this form of listing (Shoham and Lazinger, 1991).

The transition in the late nineteenth century to the card catalog enabled, on the one hand, a constantly updated catalog; on the other, it necessitated discussion and thus intellectual vacillation on the issue of the principles of cataloging, and fomented a rise in concepts of added entries along with the main entry, the central component in the rules of cataloging.

The cards indeed enabled updating, meaning more than one entry for each listed item, especially since cards are cheaper to produce than book catalogs. On the other hand, writing by hand on each card required precious work time and necessitated the widespread approach to catalog codes known as partial cataloging, under entries that were considered minor compared with an initial access point to a publication that included the full entry.

The traditional catalog was designed to serve as an index to a particular collection (although today this definition is no longer valid). Along with it there developed, although at a different historical pace, accessory tools designed to aid in location of documents and information without any connection to a specific collection.

The first of these tools is the *bibliography*. Callimachus's list may already (in the view of some scholars) have been a bibliographic list of works and not a library catalog.

Trade in books led to the emergence of book-trade bibliography, which began in the manuscript period, when posters prepared by professional scribes advertising their books were nailed to the doors of churches, universities, and taverns. With the advent of printing, similar posters were issued in printed form, usually folio size. Later came the hand list, usually printed in quarto or octavo size, which was either distributed by hand or inserted in books offered for sale at the main European book fairs (Binns, 1962).

The lists of the booksellers at the Frankfurt and Leipzig fairs in the sixteenth and seventeenth centuries were essentially bibliographies of books that had been printed in Germany. Examples include the list of 256 books arranged by subject on 19 pages that was first issued by Georg Willer, a bookseller from Augsburg, in

1564; Johannes Clessius's *Catalogi Librorum Germanicorum*, published by Peter Kopf in Frankfurt in 1602; and Georg Draudius's editions of *Bibliotheca Classica*, *Bibliotheca Exotica*, and *Bibliotheca Librorum Germanicorum Classica*, published in 1625.

In 1545, the German scientist Konrad Gesner attempted to collect in one list all of the scientific publications in the world in the Latin, Greek, and Hebrew languages; this became the *Bibliotheca Universalis*, which listed 15,000 documents. Most of the attempts in the sixteenth and seventeenth centuries involved the preparation of national bibliographies. In the seventeenth century, bibliographies according to subjects, that is, certain scientific areas, also began to appear. The bibliographies listed documents dealing with a certain area, in a certain format, and reflecting a certain culture, without reference to their physical location.

Within the bibliographies an important mediatory tool developed, namely, *indexes*, which were designed to aid in locating information about the existence of a document, without reference to its physical location. In other words, they placed the emphasis on the work itself. This mediatory tool, by providing information on the existence of the document, is an aid to intellectual accessibility.

The need for indexes stemmed from the development of a new type of publication: the periodical. The fact that each issue of a periodical included several items, together with the proliferation of periodicals in the seventeenth century – beginning with the publication of the *Journal des Scavans* in France (January 1665), and of *Philosophical Transactions* in London only a few months later (May 1665) – made the location of information difficult.

In 1867, indexing tools were first published in England, namely, the *Catalogue of Scientific Papers*; in 1882, Pool's *Index to the Periodical Literature*, which contained subject entries that were created from keywords in the titles of the journal articles indexed, was published in the United States. In 1896, the Cleveland Public Library began issuing the *Cumulative Index to a Selected List of Periodicals*, and in 1901 the H. W. Wilson Company began issuing the *Readers' Guide to the Periodical Literature*. In the twentieth century, as the periodical became a much more important type of publication, indexing services greatly proliferated, especially with the increase in the number of periodicals and in their size, offering more articles per issue.

In the 1960s, there began a process of the automation of indexes, and they became sophisticated tools of retrieval, providing instant access to media, and since 1980, are also available on CD ROMs.

An additional type of mediation is that of abstracting services. The enormous increase in the production of books throughout Europe in the sixteenth and seventeenth centuries, in part as a result of the Reformation and the Counter-Reformation, created a need for the provision of summaries of books and news about political events and scientific discoveries.

The first scientific periodical, *Journal des Scavans*, was essentially an abstracting journal, providing weekly abstracts of books, summaries of letters and decrees, and some other news. Each half-page was devoted to a book, usually new, with details about the author, title, and place of publication as well as critical evaluation.

Two other periodicals in French were later published in the Netherlands, the *Nouvelles de la république des lettres* (1684–1718) and the *Istoire des ouvrages des savans* (1687–1706, 1708–9). In 1703, the German abstracting journal *Monatlicher* began publication in Leipzig. The first abstracting and indexing journal devoted to articles in periodicals only was the *Aufrichtig und unparteyische Gedancken über die Journal* (1714–17), which covered 40 periodicals (Wellisch, 1994). During the eighteenth century, publications of this sort began to appear in England as well. A new approach was taken by the *Vollständige Einleitung in die Monaths-Schriften der Deutschen* (1747–53), a bi-monthly that offered the tables of contents of previous years' periodicals, and extracts from some of their articles.

The first discipline to have its own abstracting and indexing journals was chemistry. Professor L. F. F. von Crell, of Helmstadt and Göttingen, launched the *Chemisches Journal* in 1778.

Many of the first tools were the fruit of a single person's work; hence there were many fluctuations and short time spans for publications. Between 1880 and 1920, most of the important indexing and abstracting services that still exist today were established, usually by the professional organizations – for example, *Engineering Index* (1884), *Science Abstracts* (1897), and *Index Medicus* (1897). The number of abstracting and indexing services increased dramatically after the Second World War. In 1950, 300 existed; in 1963, over 1,500; in 1980, 2,500; in 1988, 4,000 (Wellisch, 1994). As of 1999, there are in the market some 5,500 databases and 4,600 CD ROM products (*Gale*, 1999).

Another drastic change was the transition to the electronic format, which altered the capacity for retrieval.

Also with respect to indexes and abstracts, physical format to a great extent dictated theoretical concepts, and with the transition since 1969 to computer-based data, theories have been developed that are designed to enable retrieval from the computer. The entire theory of thesauruses and the modes of constructing them have been adapted to the technical possibilities provided by the computer, and we have seen the development of sophisticated retrieval; Boolean searches; separate words within the title field, the subject field and the abstract, or the entire listing; different possibilities of truncation; focus on the number of times a term appears in a document; reference to the connections between terms within a defined range, and so on.

Encounters without Mediatory Tools

Along with the mediatory accessories that have been briefly surveyed here, there is a type of reader–document encounter that does not involve mediatory tools, an encounter that is performed by means of *browsing*, when direct access is provided to the readers (discussed in depth in **chapters 6 and 7**).

In our own era, when texts undergo digitalization, and the mediatory tools are already computerized, will browsing also turn into digital browsing on the computer screen?

Browsing is "the ability to move to a particular place in a database, casually display the information therein, and move to new information" (Kahn, 1988, p. 170). "Browsing interfaces permit users to enter databases at any point and move among and within documents looking for passages of interest" (Brewer, 1987, p. 30). Browsing is access to interrelated information; it is a heuristic search in a well-connected space of records (Fox and Palay, 1980).

Cove and Walsh (1987; 1988) extrapolate from the basic browsing strategies to their possible corollaries in the virtual library. Whereas the strategies that characterize search among shelves are search browsing, general-purpose browsing, and serendipitous browsing, the components of automated browsing are navigation, structure, and semantics.

At first glance, browsing a bookshelf is difficult to duplicate online. This area may undergo gradual processes such as the computerized bibliographic tools underwent – beginning with the transferring of manual modes of practice and only gradually and in stages adapting themselves to completely different modes of practice that altered the context of the encounter for the user – the information seeker – as well as altering the nature of the encounter using mediatory tools, that is, the bibliographic tools designed to enable the location of the information and the documents.

Although the term "browsing" is very common in the use of computerized databases, most of them are still not a substitute for traditional browsing. Indeed, browsing a list of terms on an OPAC screen is not as easy as scanning shelf signs.

It seems that to arrive at the possibility of virtual browsing, which would fulfill the same role that browsing among bookshelves fulfills, two conditions must be satisfied:

(1)   Virtual browsing will require a database structure that creates logical hierarchical connections among its components. Indeed, some solutions already exist. It is arguable that systems such as the Dewey Decimal Classification and the Universal Decimal Classification provide certain structures, even effective ones, for browsing. Introducing a classification scheme into the online retrieval environment can assist browsing because it establishes a logical approach to subject searching. Designing a class number for a work not only groups it with similar works, but gives it a place in a systematic array of related subjects (Chan and Hodges, 1990). Use of call numbers enables browsing of the bibli-

ographic records on-screen in their shelf-order. However, there are significant differences among systems. The Dewey Decimal Classification and the Universal Decimal Classification provide some, even effective, browsing structures. These two classification schemes have logical, hierarchical structures and use an expressive notation in decimal form.

(2)   The hypertext technique provides an additional answer to the need for the creation of physical links between documents, once there is some sort of logical connection between them. Surfing the Internet is one of the virtual modes of shifting among the documents – the passage from link to link.

Nevertheless, the virtual library still lacks a central characteristic of manual browsing, namely, the broader overview that the information seeker experiences with just one gaze (rather then looking at the contents in many stages) at the shelf. Essentially, with one gaze the library user is exposed to several shelves, immediately perceiving the entire nearby environment of the point at which he or she chose to begin. In light of this, Larson (1986) maintains that the solution is a visual representation of a logical database.

There have been several experimental attempts to cope with this lack. For example, Borgman et al. (1995) produced a catalog of a science library for children that models a library's physical appearance on-screen, including floor maps and visual displays of bookshelves. To browse, the child moves through the bookshelves, selecting categories by pointing and clicking with the mouse. This system is implemented without using the keyboard; the mouse is the only input device. Children select books by clicking on a book title. Here too, use is made of Dewey Decimal Classification up to six hierarchical levels (i.e., six decimals), in order to create the same link between the documents that exists physically in the traditional library. The bookshelves are named using Dewey schedule terms that match the classification number and/or terms taken from the subject headings and title words.

Pejtersen's (1992) Book House (a database of 3,500 fiction books) simulates the browsing of fiction shelves in a public library setting via an icon-based interface. When entering the system the user sees a picture of a hall, connecting to three different rooms that have books on shelves. When a room is chosen, it appears on the screen, showing people searching for books in different ways. The user can select one search strategy and thereby reach the required strategy area. When choosing and clicking on the browsing strategy, the system shifts immediately to an open-book representation with a randomly chosen book description. The browsing strategy also includes an icon version where users can browse through small pictures describing book contents. When they find a book, they see the book's cover itself.

A team from McGill University developed an alternative user interface for the university's library OPAC (PACE – Public Access Catalogue Extension), which simulates images of books and library shelves (Beheshti, Large, and Bialek, 1996). The spine of each book appears on the screen as a three-dimensional image with call number and title. Approximately ten books are displayed on one screen. When the user clicks on the spine of a book, a "title page" is displayed. However, this is not a picture of a real title page, but resembles a catalog record.

Projects such as these show an awareness among researchers as to the need to create tools that will enable digital browsing, which will eventually replace conventional physical browsing as we know it. Yet, conventional physical browsing is today a central tool for users trying to locate materials, whether for scientific research or leisure materials.

Summary

The documentation of information, brokered through different channels, and the provision of physical access to it, are the setting for the meeting of user and documents, reader and book. Throughout the ages, the spirit, the literature, the societal makeup and especially, the technological developments of different periods of history have influenced this meeting.

The physical format of documents has changed over the different periods of human history. So has the physical format of the formal channels of retrieval that facilitated the locating and retrieval of a desired document. The physical formats of both document and channel (as products of the technological developments of each historical period) have to a great degree dictated the accessibility of the document.

Since the middle of the 1960s, dramatic changes have occurred in the physical format of documents and retrieval tools, with the use of computer technology in their collection and retrieval. At first (1960s to 1980s), computer technology was applied to formal bibliographic tools, such as the library catalog, and indexing and abstracting publications. Next (1980s to early 1990s), encyclopedias, handbooks and other reference materials were digitized and made available to the public. The past few years have seen the fast growing digitization of periodicals. Books and monographs are only lately undergoing the transfer to the digitized medium. Added to this, the marriage of computer technology and telecommunications has brought documents directly to the users' home or office. We are, therefore, at the very center of the changing relationship between user and document, in the course of which the physical packaging of both document and retrieval tool have become identical. Accessibility and browsing capabilities will become virtual, subject only to future technological developments.

Bibliography

"Access to shelves? From the report of the Minneapolis Free Public Library." *Library Journal* 16, no. 6 (June 1891): 175.

Aguilar, William, "Influence of the card catalog on circulation in a small public library." *Library Resources & Technical Services* 28, no. 2 (April/June 1984): 175–84.

Ainley, Patricia and Barry Totterdell, *Alternative Arrangement: New Approaches to Public Library Stock*. London: Association of Assistant Librarians, 1982.

Andrews, Janet Columbia, "Investigation of criteria used by browsers when selecting adult fiction books in a public library." Ph.D. dissertation, Nova University, 1988.

Apted, S. M., "General purposive browsing." *Library Association Record* 73, no. 12 (Dec. 1971): 228–30.

Atkinson, Hugh C., "Classification in an unclassified world." In *Classification of Library Materials: Current and Future Potential for Providing Access*. Edited by Betty G. Bengtson and Janet Swan Hill. New York: Neal-Schuman, 1990, pp. 1–15.

Ayris, P., *The Stimulation of Creativity: A Review of the Literature Concerning the Concept of Browsing 1970–85* (CRU Working Paper; no. 5). University of Sheffield: Consultancy and Research Unit. Cited by D. Goodall, *Browsing in Public Libraries*, 1987, p. 7.

Babikow, Mary Beth, "Baltimore county public library: maximizing personnel resources through the generalist approach." In *Reorganization in the Public Library*. Edited by T. D. Webb. Phoenix, AZ: ORYX Press, 1985.

Baker, Sharon L., "Overload, browsers, and selections." *Library and Information Science* 8, no. 4 (Oct.–Dec. 1986): 315–29.

Basalla, George, *The Evolution of Technology*. Cambridge, England: Cambridge University Press, 1988.

Bates, Marcia J., "The design of browsing and berrypicking technique for the online search interface." *Online Review* 13, no. 5 (Oct. 1989): 407–24.

Bates, Marcia J., "Search techniques." *Annual Review of Information Science and Technology* V. 16. White Plains, N.Y.: Knowledge Industry Pub. 1981, pp. 139–69.

Baumann, Charles H., *The Influence of Agnus Snead Macdonald and the Snead Bookstack on Library Architecture*. Metuchen, N.J.: Scarecrow Press, 1972.

Becker, Joseph, "Telecommunication primer." *Journal of Library Automation* 2, no. 3 (Sept. 1969): 148–56.

Beheshti, J., "Browsing through public access catalogs." *Information Technology and Libraries* 11, no. 3 (Sept. 1992): 220–8.

Beheshti, Jamshid, Valerie Large, and Mary Bialek, "PACE: a browsable graphical interface." *Information Technology and Libraries* 15, no. 4 (Dec. 1996): 231–40.

Bell, Daniel, *The Coming of the Post-Industrial Revolution: A Venture in Social Forecasting*. New York: Basic Books, 1973.

Beniger, James R., *The Control Revolution: Technological and Economic Origins of the Information Society*. Cambridge, Mass.: Harvard University Press, 1986.

Bermant, Chaim and Michael Weitzman, *Ebla: A Revelation in Archeology*. New York: Times Books, 1979.

Best, Gordon, "Direction-finding in large buildings." In *Architectural Psychology: Proceedings of the Conference Held at Dalandhui, University of Strathclyde, 28 February–2 March 1969*. Edited by D. V. Canter. London: RIBA Publications, 1969, pp. 72–5.

Binns, Norman E., *An Introduction to Historical Bibliography*. 2nd edn. London: Association of Assistant Librarians, 1962.

Bishop, W. W., "The historical development of library buildings." In *Library Buildings for Library Service: Papers Presented before the Library Institute at the University of Chicago, August 5–10, 1946*. Edited by Herman H. Fussler. Chicago: American Association, 1947.

Bliss, Henry Evelyn, *The Organization of Knowledge in Libraries, and the Subject Approach to Books*. 2nd edn. New York: Wilson Com., 1939.

Boll, John J., "Shelf browsing, open access and storage capacity in research libraries." *Occasional Papers* No. 169 (June 1985). University of Illinois, Urbana, Graduate School of Library and Information Science, 1985.

Borgman, Albert, *Technology and the Character of Contemporary Life: A Philosophical Inquiry*. Chicago: University of Chicago Press, 1984.

Borgman, Christine L. et al., "Children's searching behavior on browsing and keyword online catalogs: the Science Library Catalog Project." *Journal of the American Society for Information Science* 46, no. 9 (1995): 663–84.

Bosman, Ellen and Carol Rusinek, "Creating the user-friendly library by evaluating patron perceptions on signage." *Reference Services Review* 25, no. 1 (1997): 71–82.

Bostick, Sharon Lee, "The development and validation of the library anxiety scale." Ph.D. dissertation, Wayne State University, 1992.

Bostwick, Arthur E., *The American Public Library*. New York: D. Appleton, 1917.

Bowen, Alice, "Non-recorded use of books and browsing in the stacks of a research library." Master's thesis, University of Chicago, 1961. Cited by Richard Joseph Hyman, *Access to Library Collections*, 1972, pp. 43–6.

Brewer, Bryan, "The look and feel and sound of the user interface." *CD-ROM Review* 2, no. 3 (July / Aug. 1987): 26–30.

British Museum, *The Catalogue of Printed Books in the British Museum*. London, 1841.

Broadbent, Elaine, "A study of humanities faculty library information seeking behavior." *Cataloging and Classification Quarterly* 6, no. 3 (Spring 1986): 23–37.

Brown, Eleanor Frances, *Library Service to the Disadvantaged*. Metuchen, N.J.: Scarecrow Press, 1971.

Buckland, Michael K., *Library Services in Theory and Context*. 2nd edn. New York: Pergamon Press, 1988.

Butler, Samuel, *The Works of Samuel Butler: Canterbury Settlement*. New York: AMS Press, 1968.

Buzás, Ladislaus, *German Library History, 800–1945*. Jefferson, N.C.: McFarland, 1986.

Celoria, F., "The archeology of serendip." *Library Association Record* 70, no. 10 (1968): 251–5.

Chan, L. M. and T. Hodges, "Subject cataloging and classification:

the late 1980s and beyond." In *Technical Services Today and Tomorrow*. Edited by M. Gorman et al. Englewood, Colo.: Libraries Unlimited, 1990, pp. 74–85.

Christeusen, John O., "Management of popular reading collections." *Collection Management* 6, nos. 3–4 (Fall/Winter 1984): 8.

Clark, John Willis, *The Care of Books: An Essay on the Development of Libraries and Their Fittings from the Earliest Times to the End of the Eighteenth Century*. Cambridge: Cambridge University Press, 1902.

Clark, J. W., *Libraries in the Medieval and Renaissance Periods*. Chicago: Argonaut, 1894.

Classification of Library Materials: Current and Future Potential for Providing Access. Edited by G. Bengtson and Janet Swan Hill. New York: Neal-Schuman, 1990.

Cochrane, P. and K. Markey, "Preparing for the use of classification in online cataloging systems and in online catalogs." *Information Technology & Libraries* 4, no. 2 (June 1985): 91–111.

Conmy, Peter T., "William Howard Brett: Apostle of Good Faith in Public Librarianship." *American Libraries* 6, no. 8 (Sept. 1975): 465.

Cooper, Michael D., "The sensitivity of book storage strategy decisions to alternative cost assumptions." *Library Quarterly* 61, no. 4 (Oct. 1991): 415–28.

Cooper, Michael D. and John Wolthausen, "Misplacement of books on library shelves: a mathematical model." *Library Quarterly* 47, no. 1 (Jan. 1977): 43–57.
Cove, Joanne Frances and B. C. Walsh, "Browsing as a means of online text retrieval." *Information Services and Use* 7, no. 6 (1987): 183–8.

Cove, J. F. and B. C. Walsh, "Online text retrieval via browsing." *Information Processing and Management* 24, no. 1 (1988): 31–7.

Cutter, C. A., "Close classification: with special reference to Messrs, Perkins, Schwartz, and Dewey." *Library Journal* XI, no. 7 (July 1886): 180–4.

Cutter, C. A., *Expansive Classification*. Part I. *The First Six Classification*. Boston: The Author, 1891–3.

Cutter, C. A., *Rules for a Dictionary Catalog*. 4th edn. Washington: Government Printing Office, 1904.

Dewey, Melvil, "Arrangement on the shelves." *Library Journal* 4, no. 6 (June 30, 1879): 191–4.

Dewey, Melvil, *Decimal Classification and Relative Index*. 2nd edn. Revised and greatly enlarged. Boston: Library Bureau, 1885.

Dewey, Melvil, "Introduction," 10th edn. 1926. In *Dewey Decimal Classification*. 17th edn. New York: Forest Press, 1965, pp. 63–108.

Drabenstott, Karen Markey et al., "Analysis of a bibliographic database enhanced with a library classification." *Library Resources & Technical Services* 34, no. 2 (April 1990): 179–98.

Drucker, Peter F., "The coming of the new organization." *Harvard Business Review* (Jan.–Feb. 1988): 45–53.

Dunkin, Paul S., *Cataloging U.S.A.* Chicago: ALA, 1969.

Eaton, Gale, "Wayfinding in the library: book searches and route uncertainty." *RQ* 30, no. 4 (Summer 1991): 519–27.
Ellis, David, "The behavioral model of information retrieval system for information retrieval design." *Journal of Information Science* 15, nos. 4/5 (1989): 237–47.

Ellis, David, "Theory and explanation in information retrieval research." *Journal of Information Science* 8, no. 1 (Feb. 1984): 25–38.

Ellsworth, R. E., *Academic Library Buildings: A Guide to Architectural Issues and Solutions*. Boulder, Colo.: Colorado Associated University Press, 1973.

Ellsworth, Ralph E., *Planning the College and University Library Building: A Book for Campus Planners and Architects*. 2nd edn. Boulder, Colo.: Pruett Press, 1968.

Erünsal, Ismail E., "Ottoman libraries: a brief survey of their development and system of lending." *Libri* 34, no. 1 (March 1984): 65–76.

Feenberg, Andrew, "Subversive rationalization: technology, power, and democracy." In *Technology and the Politics of Knowledge*. Edited by Andrew Feenberg and Alastair Hannay. Bloomington: Indiana University Press, 1995, pp. 3–22.

Fox, Mark S. and Andrew J. Palay, "Machine-assisted browsing for the naive user." In *Public Access to Library Automation: Papers Presented at the 1980 Clinic on Library Applications of Data Processing, April 20–23, 1980*, pp. 77–98.

Franklin, Alfred, *Les Anciennes Bibliothèques de Paris: Eglises, Monastères, Collèges, etc.* (Histoire Générale de Paris: Collection de documents). Paris: Imprimerie Impériale, 1867.

Franklin, Alfred, *La Sorbonne: ses origines, sa bibliothèque, les débuts de l'imprimerie à Paris et la succession de Richelieu d'après des documents inédits*. Amsterdam: Gerard Th. Van Heusden, 1986 (reprint of Paris edition, 1875).

Frost, Carolyn O., "The Bodleian catalogs of 1674 and 1738: an examination in the light of modern cataloging theory." *Library Quarterly* 46, no. 3 (July 1976): 248–70.

Fussler, Herman H. and Julian L. Simon, *Patterns in the Use of*

Books in Large Research Libraries. Chicago: University of Chicago Press, 1969.

Gale Directory of Databases. Edited by Lisa Kumar. V. 1: Online databases; V. 2: CD-ROM diskette, magnetic tape, handheld and batch access database products. Detroit: Gale Group, March 1999.

Garnett, Emily, "Reference service by telephone." *Library Journal* 61 (Dec. 1, 1936): 909–11.

Give'em What They Want. The Baltimore County Public Library's Blue Ribbon Committee. Chicago: American Library Association, 1992.

Goldhor, Herbert, "The effect of prime display location on public library circulation of selected adult titles." *Library Quarterly* 42, no. 4 (Oct. 1972): 371–89.

Goldhor, Herbert, "Experimental effects on the choice of books borrowed by public library adult patrons." *Library Quarterly* 51, no. 3 (Oct. 1981): 253–68.

Goodall, Deborah L., "Use made of adult fiction collection (Arnold Library, Nottinghamshire)." BA dissertation, Department of Library and Information Studies, Loughborough University, 1987.

Goodall, Deborah, *Browsing in Public Libraries* (LISU Occasional Paper; no. 1). Loughborough: Library and Information Statistics Unit, 1989.

Goodall, Deborah, "Browsing in public libraries in Derbyshire." Unpublished report using data collected by the Centre for Library and Information Management, Loughborough University, Library and Information Statistics Unit, 1988.

Gordon, Harold, "Open stacks: a second look." *Library Journal* 94, no. 9 (May 1, 1969): 1844–5.

Gore, Daniel, *Bibliography for Beginners*. 2nd edn. New York: Appleton-Century-Crofts, 1973.

Greene, Robert J., "The effectiveness of browsing." *College & Research Libraries* 38, no. 4 (July 1977): 313–16.

Gyeszly, Suzanne D., "Computer aided storage design." *Technical Services Quarterly* 8, no. 1 (1990): 51–9.

Hancock-Beaulieu, Micheline, "Evaluating the impact of an online library catalogue on subject searching behaviour at the catalogue and at the shelves." *Journal of Documentation* 46, no. 4 (Dec. 1990): 318–38.

Hancock, Micheline, "Subject searching behaviour at the library catalogue and at the shelves: implications for online interactive catalogues." *Journal of Documentation* 43, no. 4 (Dec. 1987): 303–21.

Hansson, Joachim, "Why public libraries in Sweden did not choose Dewey." *Knowledge Organization* 24, no. 3 (1997): 145–53.

Harris, C., "A comparison of issues and in-library use of books." *ASLIB Proceedings* 29, no. 3 (March 1977): 118–26.

Harris, Michael H., *History of Libraries in the Western World*. 4th edn. Lanham, Md.: Scarecrow Press, 1995.

Harrison, Kim M., "Paperback books in public libraries." MA dissertation, Department of Library and Information Studies, Loughborough University, 1984.

Herner, Saul, "Browsing." In *Encyclopedia of Library and Information Science*. V. 3 (1970): 408–15.

Herner, Saul, "A pilot study of the use of the stacks of the Library of Congress." Washington, D.C., 1960 (Typewritten). Cited by Hyman, *Access to Library Collections*, 1972, pp. 38–41.

Hildreth, Charles (a), "The concept and mechanics of browsing in an online library catalog." In *National Online Meeting: Proceedings – 1982*. Compiled by Martha E. Williams, Thomas H. Hogan. Medford, N.J.: Learned Information, 1982, pp. 181–96.

Hildreth, Charles R. (b), "Online browsing support capabilities." In *Proceedings of the ASIS Annual Meeting, Columbus, Ohio, Oct. 17–21, 1982.* V. 19 (1982): 127–32.

Hosmer, James K., "On browsing by a book-worm." *Library Journal* 15, no. 12 (Dec. 1890): 33–7.

Hyman, Richard Joseph, *Access to Library Collections: An Inquiry into the Validity of the Direct Shelf Approach, with Special Reference to Browsing.* Netuchen, N.J.: Scarecrow Press, 1972.

Hyman, Richard J., "Access to library collections: summary of a documentary and opinion survey on the direct shelf approach and browsing." *Library Resources & Technical Services* 15, no. 4 (Fall 1971): 479–91.

Hyman, Richard Joseph, *Shelf Access in Libraries.* Chicago: American Library Association, 1982.

Hyman, Richard J., "Shelf classification research: past, present – future." *Occasional Papers* No. 146 (Nov. 1980). University of Illinois, Urbana, Graduate School of Library Science, 1980.

Jackson, Sidney L., *Catalog Use Study.* Edited by Vaclav Mostecky. Chicago: ALA, 1958.

Jennings, B. and L. Sear, "Readers select fiction" (Kent County Library and development Report; no. 9). Kent County Council, Education Committee, 1986.

Jiao, Qun G. and Anthony J. Onwuegbuzie, "Antecedents of library anxiety." *Library Quarterly* 67, no. 4 (1997): 372–89.

Johnson, Elmer D., *History of Libraries in the Western World.* 2nd edn. Metuchen, N.J.: Scarecrow Press, 1970.

Kahn, Paul, "Making a difference: a review of the user interface features in six CD-ROM database products." *Optical Information Systems* 8, no. 4 (July–Aug 1988): 169–83.

Kaser, David, "Foreword." In Dorothy Pollet and Peter C. Haskell, *Sign Systems for Libraries: Solving the Wayfinding Problem.* New York: Bowker, 1979, pp. vii–viii.

Kaser, D. "The American Academic Library Building, 1870–1890." In *Libraries, Books and Culture: Proceedings of Library History Seminar, VII, 6–8 March 1985, Chapel Hill, North Carolina.* Edited by Donald G. Davis. Austin, Tex.: Graduate School of Library and Information Science, University of Texas at Austin, 1986.

Kelley, Grace Osgood, *The Classification of Books: An Inquiry into Its Usefulness to the Reader.* New York: Wilson, 1937.

Khristova, Boryana, "Bibliotekata na Rilskiya Manastir [The Rila Monastery library]." *Bibliotekar* 30, no. 12 (1983): 10–13.

Knuston, Gunnar, "Does the catalog record make a difference? Access points and book use." *College & Research Libraries* 47, no. 5 (Sept. 1986): 460–9.

Large, J. A., "The libraries of the Carthusian Order in Medieval England." *Library History* 3, no. 6 (Autumn 1975): 191–203.

Larsson, H., *Tidstecken: Stockholms Arbetarbibliotek ock Samballskroppens Utforming 1892–1927* [Signs of the Time: Stockholm Workers' Library and the Shape of Society 1892–1927]. Stockholm: Kommitten for stockholmsforskning, 1989. Cited by J. Hansson, "Why public libraries in Sweden did not choose Dewey." *Knowledge Organization* 24, no. 3 (1997), p. 147.

Larson, James A., "A visual approach to browsing in a database environment." *Computer* 19, no. 6 (June 1986): 62–71.

LeBlanc, Jim, "Classification and shelf listing as value added: some remarks on the relative worth and price of predictability, serendipity, and depth of access." *Library & Resources Technical Services* 39, no. 3 (July 1995): 294–302.

Licklider, J. C. R., "Proposed experiments in browsing." In *INTREX: Report of a Planning Conference on Information Transfer Experiments*. Edited by Carl F. J. Overhange and R. Joyce Harman. Cambridge, Mass.: MIT Press, 1965, pp. 187–97.

London, Jack, *The Call of the Wild*. New York: Macmillan, 1903.

Long, Sarah P., "The effect of face-front book display in the public library." *North Carolina Libraries* 45 (Fall 1987): 150–3.

Losee, Robert M., "A gray code based ordering for documents on shelves: classification for browsing and retrieval." *Journal of the American Society of Information Science* 43, no. 4 (May 1992): 312–22.

Losee, Robert M., "The relative shelf location of circulated books: a study of classification, users, and browsing." *Library Resources & Technical Services* 37, no. 2 (April 1993): 197–209.

Lowell, James Russell, *Among My Books*. Boston: J. R. Books, 1873.

Luckham, Bryan, *The Library in Society: A Study of the Public Library in an Urban setting*. London: Library Association, 1971.

Malinconico, S. Michael, "Librarians and innovation: an American viewpoint." *Program* 31, no. 1 (Jan. 1997): 47–58.

Malinconico, S. Michael, "Technology and standards for bibliographic control." *Library Quarterly* 47, no. 3 (1977): 308–25.
Maltby, Arthur and Eric Hunter, "Readers and classification." *New Library World* 73, no. 868 (Oct. 1972): 411–13.

Maltby, Arthur, *Sayers' Manual of Classification for Librarians and Bibliographers*, 5th edn. London: Andre Deutsch, 1975.

Mann, Thomas, *Catalog and Classification Quality at the Library of Congress*. Washington, D.C.: Library of Congress, 1994.
Marchionini, Gary, "An invitation to browse: designing full-text systems for novice users." *Canadian Journal of Information Science* 12, nos. 3–4 (1987): 69–79.

Marks, Susan, "Browsing room redivivus (flow of function in libraries)." *American Libraries* 7, no. 2 (Feb. 1976): 94–5.

Marsterson, W. A. J., "Users of libraries: a comparative study." *Journal of Librarianship* 6, no. 2 (Apr. 1974): 63–79.

Massicotte, Mia, "Improved browsable displays for online subject access." *Information Technology and Libraries* 7, no. 4 (Dec. 1988): 373–80.

Mellon, Constance A., "Library anxiety: a grounded theory and its development." *College and Research Libraries* 47, no. 2 (March 1986): 160–5.

Micklewright, G. R., "An arrangement of fiction." *Library World* 37, no. 7 (1935): 156–7.

Morse, Philip M., "Browsing and search theory." In *Toward a Theory of Librarianship: Papers in Honor of Jesse Hauk Shera*. Edited by Conrad H. Rawski. Metuchen, N.J.: Scarecrow Press, 1973, pp. 246–61.

Morse, Philip M., "Search theory and browsing." *Library Quarterly* 40, no. 3 (July 1970): 391–408.

Musmann, Klaus, *Technological Innovation in Libraries, 1860–1960: An Anecdotal History*. Westport, Conn.: Greenwood Press, 1993.

Naudé, Gabriel, *Advice on Establishing a Library* [translation of: *Avis pour dresser une bibliothèque*, 1627]. Berkeley: University of California Press, 1950.

Nichols, Elizabeth Dickinson, "Classification decision-making in California libraries." In *Classification of Library Materials: Current and Future Potential for Providing Access*. Edited by Betty G. Bengtson and Janet Swan Hill. New York: Neal-Shuman, 1990, pp. 146–73.

Nissen, Hans J., *The Early History of the Ancient Near East 9000–2000 BC*. Chicago: University of Chicago Press, 1988.

Norris, Dorothy May, *A History of Cataloging and Cataloging Methods 1100–1850; With an Introductionary Survey of Ancient Times*. London: Grafton, 1939.

Oddy, R. N., "Information retrieval through man–machine dialogue." *Journal of Documentation* 33, no. 1 (March 1977): 1–14.

Onwuegbuzie, Anthony J., "Writing a research proposal: the role of library anxiety, statistics anxiety, and composition anxiety." *Library and Information Science Research* 19, no. 1 (1997): 5–33.

Parr, Virginia H., "Case study: a collection development policy for an academic library endowed enrichment area and collection." *Collection Management* 6, nos. 3–4 (Fall/Winter 1984): 83–92.

Parsons, Edward Alexander, *The Alexandrian Library: Glory of the Hellenic World: Its Rise, Antiquities, and Destruction*. Amsterdam: Elsevier Press, 1952.

Pejtersen, A. M., "New model for multimedia interfaces to online public access catalogues." *The Electronic Library* 10, no. 6 (Dec. 1992): 359–66.
Pitt-Rivers, Augustus Lane-Fox, *The Evolution of Culture and Other Essays*. Oxford: Clarendon Press, 1906.

Poole, William F., "Organization and management of the public library." In U.S. Bureau of Education, *Public Libraries in the United States*, 1876, pp. 476–504.

Posner, Ernst, *Archives in the Ancient World*. Cambridge, Mass.: Harvard University Press, 1972.
Poulter, Alan, "Browsing the virtual library." In *Encyclopedia of Library and Information Science* V. 62, supplement 25. New York: Marcel Dekker, 1998, pp. 54–64.

Putnam, Herbert, "Access to the shelves, a possible function of branch libraries." *Library Journal* 16, no. 12 (Dec. 1891): 62–7.

Ranganathan, S. R., "Colon classification and its approach to documentation." In *Bibliographic Organization: Papers Presented before the 15th Annual Conference of the Graduate Library School, July 24–29, 1950.* Edited by Jesse H. Shera and Margaret E. Egan. Chicago: University of Chicago Press, 1951, pp. 94–105.

Ranganathan, S. R., *Elements of Library Classification.* Bombay: Asia Publishing House, 1962.

Ranganathan, S. R., *Theory of Library Catalogue.* Madras: Madras Library Association, 1938.

Ranz, Jim, *The Printed Book Catalogue in American Libraries 1723–1900.* Chicago: ALA, 1964.

Reichman, Felix, "The catalog in European libraries." In *Library Catalogs: Changing Dimensions.* Edited by Ruth French Strout. Chicago: University of Chicago Press, 1964, pp. 34–56.

Ricarda, M., "1948 survey of browsing rooms." *Catholic Library World* 20 (1949): 242–6.
Richardson, Ernest Cushing, *The Beginning of Libraries.* Handen, Conn.: Archon Books, 1963. (Originally published in 1914.)

Robinson, Otis H., "College library administration." In U.S. Bureau of Education, *Public Libraries in the United States,* 1876, pp. 505–25.

Ross, Johnson, "Observations of browsing behavior in an academic library." *College & Research Libraries* 44, no. 4 (July 1983): 269–76.
Rovelstad, Mathilde, "Open shelves/closed shelves in research libraries." *College & Research Libraries* 37, no. 5 (Sept. 1976): 457–67.

Ryan, Sara, "Reference service for the Internet community: a case study of the Internet Public Library reference Division." *Library and Information Science Research* 18, no. 3 (Summer 1996): 241–59.

Sawdridge, L. and T. L. Favret, "The mechanism and magic of declassification." *Library Association Record* 84, no. 11 (1982): 385–6.

Schlereth, Thomas J., ed., *Material Culture Studies in America*. Nashville, Tenn.: American Association for State and Local History, 1982.

Sear, Lyn and Barbara Jennings, *How Readers Select Fiction* (Kent County Library Research and Development; Report no. 9). Education Committee, Kent County Council, 1986.

Selth, Jeff, Nancy Koller, and Peter Briscoe, "The use of books within the library." *College & Research Libraries* 53, no. 3 (May 1992): 197–205.

Shelton, Regina, "The lure of the browsing room." *Library Journal* 107, no. 4 (Feb. 15, 1982): 410–13.

Shoham, Snunith and Susan S. Lazinger, "The no-main entry principle and the automated catalog." *Cataloging & Classification Quarterly* 12, nos. 3–4 (1991): 51–67.

Slater, Margaret and Pamela Fisher, *Use Made of Technical Libraries* (ASLIB Occasional Publication; 2). London: ASLIB, 1969.

Spenceley, Nicholas, "The readership of literary fiction: a survey of library users in the Sheffield area." MA dissertation, Postgraduate School of Librarianship, Sheffield University, 1980.

Sperry, John A. Jr., "Egyptian libraries: a survey of the evidence." *Libri* 7, nos. 2–3 (1957): 145–55.

Spiller, David, "The provision of fiction for public libraries." *Journal of Librarianship* 12, no. 4 (Oct. 1980): 238–66.

Steptowe, Catherine C., "A case-study of fiction provision in a public library." MA dissertation, Department of Library and Information Studies, Loughborogh University, 1987.

Stevens, Rolland E., "The study of the research use of libraries." *Library Quarterly* 26, no. 1 (Jan. 1956): 41–51.

Stone, Sue, "Humanities scholars: information needs and uses." *Journal of Documentation* 38, no. 4 (Dec. 1982): 292–313.

Streeter, Burnett Hillman, *The Chained Library: A Survey of Four Centuries in the Evolution of the English Library.* London: Macmillan, 1931.

Strout, Ruth French, "The development of the catalog and cataloging codes." In *Toward a Better Cataloging Code.* Edited by Ruth French Strout. Chicago: University of Chicago, Graduate Library School, 1956, pp. 4–25.

Svenonius, Elaine, "Directions for research in indexing, classification, and cataloging." *Library Resources & Technical Services* 25, no. 1 (Jan./March 1981): 88–103.
Thompson, E. Margaret, *The Carthusian Order in England.* London: Society for Promoting Christian Knowledge, 1930.

Thompson, James Westfall, *Ancient Libraries.* 1940 (reprint: Hamden, Conn.: Archon, 1962).

Thompson, James Westfall, *The Medieval Library.* Chicago: University of Chicago Press, 1939.
Toffler, Alvin, *Future Shock.* New York: Bantam Books, 1971.

Turner, Susan E., "A survey of borrowers' reaction to literary fiction, Beeston Library, Nottinghamshire." MA dissertation, Department of Library and Information Studies, Loughborough University, 1987.

United States Bureau of Education, *Public Libraries in United the States of America: Their History, Condition, and Management: Special*

Report. Part I. Washington: Government Printing Office, 1876.

Urquart, D. J., "National lending/reference libraries or libraries of first resort." *BLL Review* 4, no. 1 (1976): 7–10.

Verona, Eva, "Literary unit versus bibliographical unit." *Libri* 9, no. 2 (1959): 79–104.

Vig, Norman J., "Technology, philosophy, and the state: an overview." In *Technology and Politics*. Edited by Michael E. Kraft and Norman J. Vig. Durham, N.C.: Duke University Press, 1998.
Voigt, Melvin J., "The researcher and his sources of scientific information." *Libri* 9, no. 3 (1959): 177–93.

Wakeham, M., "Nurses – their information needs and use of libraries: the view of some librarians." *Health Libraries Review* 10, no. 2 (June 1993): 85–94.

Ward, M. L., *Readers and Library Users: A Study of Reading Habits and Public Library Use*. London: Library Association, 1977.
Warren, S. R. and S. N. Clark, "College Libraries." In U.S. Bureau of Education, *Public Libraries in the United States*, 1876, pp. 60–126.

Weber, Max, *Essays in Sociology*. Oxford: Oxford University Press, 1964.

Webster's Third New International Dictionary of the English Language Unabridged. Springfield, Mass.: Merriam-Webster, 1961.

Weisman, Jerry, "Evaluating architectural legibility: wayfinding in the built environment." *Environment and Behavior* 13 (March 1981): 189–203.

Weitemeyer, Mogens, "Archive and library technique in ancient Mesopotamia." *Libri* 6, no. 3 (1956): 217–38.

Wellisch, Hans H., "Abstracting and indexing services." In *Encyclopedia of Library History*. Edited by Wayne A. Wiegand and

Donlald G. Davis, Jr. New York: Garland Pub., 1994, pp. 2–5.

Wheeler, Joseph Lewis and Alfred Morton Githens, *The American Public Library Building: Its Planning and Design with Special Reference to Its Administration and Service*. Chicago: ALA, 1959. (Reprint: Ann Arbor, Mich.: University Microfilms International, 1978.)

Wheeler, Joseph Lewis, *Wheeler and Goldhor's Practical Administration of Public Libraries*. New York: Harper & Row, 1981.

Willard, Patricia and Viva Teece, "The browser and the library." *Public Library Quarterly* 4, no. 1 (Spring 1983): 55–63.

Willard, Patricia and Viva Teece, "Satisfying the user: a look at a local public library." *Australian Library Journal* 32, no. 1 (Feb. 1983): 41–6.

Winsor, Justin, "Library building." In U.S. Bureau of Education, *Public Library in the United States*, 1876, pp. 465–75.
Witty, Francis J., "The other Pinakes and reference works on Callimachus." *Library Quarterly* 43, no. 3 (July 1973): 237–44.

Witty, Francis J., "The Pinakes of Callimachus." *Library Quarterly* 28, no. 2 (April 1958): 132–6.

Wood, D. N., "Local acquisition and discarding policies in the light of national library resources and services." *Aslib Proceedings* 29, no. 1 (Jan. 1977): 24–34.
Young, A. Beatrice, "The recreational reading room." *Journal of Higher Education* 13 (1942): 434–7.

Younger, Jennifer, "Classification and the library user." In *Classification of Library Materials: Current Future Potential for Providing Access*. Edited by Betty G. Bergston and Janet Swan Hill. New York: Neal Schuman Pub., 1990, pp. 174–81.

Index

---

abstracting services and journals, 84, 106, 109, 132–3, 137
academic libraries. *See* college and university libraries
accessibility, viii, 8, 29, 31, 57, 58, 61–2, 63, 65, 67, 68, 72–3, 75, 76, 116, 123, 124–5, 137
See also open-shelf system
Academy Nauk (Leningrad), library, 44
Adonis project, 9
Alexandrian library, 17, 35, 55, 125
architecture, of libraries, 8, 23, 24–7, 28, 29, 30–1, 76–8, 88
Ambrosian library. *See* Bibliotheca Ambrosiana
ARIEL, 10
Aristotle, 35, 57
Armaria (presses), 17, 19–20, 24, 30, 58
arrangement of library materials, viii, 8, 33–4, 36–7, 38, 39, 43–7, 48–9, 50, 51, 52, 53–4, 55–6, 61, 65, 67, 75, 80, 82, 83, 84, 88, 89, 95, 99, 104, 117, 125, 126, 128
See also classification (methods and systems); closed stacks system; open-shelf system; shelves and shelving
Assur-bani-pal, 7, 15, 34, 54, 57

Babylonian libraries. *See* Mespotamian libraries
Baltimore County Public Library, 51
Bavarian Royal library (Munich), 28
Benedictine libraries, 19, 23, 59, 126

Bexley Public Library (England), 52
Bibliographic Classification, 48, 86
Bibliothèque Nationale (Paris), 10, 44
Bibliothèque Mazarine (Paris), 26, 41, 62
bibliographies, 84, 107, 125, 130, 131
Bibliotheca Ambrosiana (Milan), 26, 62
Bliss, Henry Evelyn, 48, 86
Bodleian Library, 24, 25, 26, 39, 62, 127
bookcases. *See* shelves and shelving
Boston Public Library, 27, 28, 49, 51, 64, 66
borrowing. *See* circulation
Brett, William, Howard, 67
British Museum, 10, 28, 44
Brooklyn Public Library (New York), 49, 51
Brown University, library catalog, 128
browsing, viii, 54, 65, 66, 70, 71, 78, 81, 82, 83, 84, 88, 91, 93, 94–5,104, 105, 106, 107, 108, 110, 111, 112, 114–17, 118, 120, 123, 133, 134
and collection building, 80
the card catalog, 96, 100
and classification. *See* classification and browsing (or as a locational device)
definitions, 91, 93, 96, 97–101, 103
effectiveness, 116–19
in academic libraries. *See* college and academic libraries, and browsing in public libraries. *See* Public libraries, and browsing

the online catalog, 91, 94,100
   among the shelves, 31, 47, 66, 78,
      79, 81–2, 84, 86, 87, 88, 91, 92, 93,
      94, 95, 96, 99, 100, 104, 106, 107,
      108, 109, 110–11, 113, 115, 119,
      120, 134, 135, 136
   techniques, 94, 96, 97, 98, 99,
      100–1, 134
   virtual browsing, 133, 134, 136,
      137
browsing rooms and areas, 30, 51, 57,
      58, 64, 67–8, 70, 73, 82, 85, 113,
      114, 120, 124–5
Buffalo Public Library , 49

Callimachus, 35, 36, 125, 130
Cambridge Public Library
      (Massachusetts), 49
Cambridgeshire Public Library
      (England), 53
Cambridge University (England),
      libraries, 22, 24, 25, 26, 61
Cassiodorus, 19
cataloging codes, 12, 127, 128–9
catalogs, 11, 12, 20, 34, 43, 45, 47, 65,
      67, 69, 84, 99, 100, 106, 107, 108,
      117, 120, 125, 126, 128, 135
   author, 44, 126, 127
   automated, 12, 94, 110, 120, 128,
      129, 137. See also Online Public
      Access Catalog
   book, 129
   card, 11, 12, 93, 95, 96, 100, 106,
      112, 130
   classified, 87, 127
   as a collocative device, 128
   computerized See catalogs, auto-
      mated
   dictionary, 86
   as a finding list, 126, 127–8
   Medieval, 20, 21, 30, 36, 126–7
   microform, 12
   online. See catalogs, automated as
      a shelf list, 36
   single entry , 129–30
   subject, 86, 87, 126, 127
   union, 126
   See also under specific libraries
cathedral libraries, 23, 25, 26, 37, 38,
      55

CD ROMs 9, 120, 132, 133
chaining of books, 20, 24, 25, 30, 61,
      62, 63, 72, 124
Cheshire Public Library (England),
      53
Chicago Public Library, 51
children's books, 49–50, 54
circulation, 27, 46, 59, 60, 61, 62, 68,
      70, 72, 75, 78, 79, 80, 81–2, 85, 89,
      92, 105, 107, 108, 109, 110, 111,
      112, 113, 117, 119, 124
Citeaux, monastery at, library, 21
   catalog, 21
classification, and browsing, 82, 84,
      94, 95, 104, 134
   as a locational device, 46, 85, 86–8
   methods and systems, viii, 33, 35,
      36, 38, 39, 40–3, 44, 45, 46, 47, 48,
      52, 56, 65, 82, 84, 85, 86, 87, 99,
      104, 117, 134
clay boards. See clay tablets
clay tablets, 7, 10, 11, 12, 15, 16, 30,
      33, 34, 55, 57, 72, 125
Clerkenwell Library (London), 70
Clessius, Johannes, 131
Cleveland Public Library, 28, 49, 50,
      51, 66, 67
closed-shelf system, 44, 45, 56, 58, 64,
      68, 70, 72, 73, 92, 124
closed stacks. See closed-shelf system
codices, 11, 12, 17, 20, 30
collection-building, 75, 80–1
college and university libraries, 22–3,
      25, 28, 29, 39, 48, 55, 60, 62, 64, 69,
      71, 72, 77, 79, 82, 87, 124
   and browsing, 98, 106, 108, 109,
      117
   See also under specific universities
Colon Classification, 48, 86
Columbus Public Library, 66
communication technologies, 5, 125,
      137
Court Library (Vienna), 43
Christ Church (Canterbury), library,
      21
Copenhagen University, library, 25
Cutter, Charles Ami, 46, 65, 67, 128,
      129

Demetrius of Phaleron, 17, 35

Detroit Public Library, 51, 54
Dewey Decimal Classification, 46, 47, 52, 54, 56, 65, 85, 86, 134–5
Dewey, Melvill, 46–8, 56, 65
Diechman Public Library (Oslo), 70–1
direct access to books. *See* open-shelf system
Draudius, Georg, 131
Durham, library, 20, 21, 59
    catalog, 20–1, 59

Ebla, library of, 15
    catalog, 34
Edfu, library of, 34, 125
Edinburgh University, library, 25
Egyptian libraries, 33, 34, 57
Enoch Pratt Free Library (Baltimore), 28
Escorial library (Spain), 26

Feuillant monastery (Paris), 127
fiction books, 49, 50, 51, 53, 54, 68, 93, 111, 112, 113, 136
Free Library of Philadelphia, 68
Free Library of Pawtucket (Rhode Island), 66
French Code of 1791, 127
furniture, library, 88
    See also under specific type of furniture, e.g., armaria, lectern-system library, stall-system library, etc.

galleries, 27
Genser, Konrad, 131
Georgia Institute of Technology, library, 106, 118
Greek libraries, 17, 19, 35, 36, 55, 57, 58, 124
Georgetown College, library, 64
Gutenberg, Johannes, 7

hall-type libraries, 27, 62, 72
Harvard college, library catalog, 128
Harvard University, 69
Hoddesdon Public Library (England), 54

ILL. *See* inter-library loan services
indexes, 84, 95, 106, 110, 128, 131–2, 133, 137

Indiana University Northwest, 77
Industrial Revolution, 4, 6
information-retrieval behavior. *See* information-seeking behavior
information-seeking behavior, 13, 77, 98, 99, 103, 106, 107, 113, 114, 115, 120, 134
    of humanistic scholars, 109, 110, 120, 121
    of social scientists, 109, 110, 120
    of scientists , 110, 120–1
information-use strategies, 103, 104
inter-library loan services, 9, 60
Internet time, 6, 8
Isidore of Seville, library of, 36

Jesuits' library (France), 26
Jewett, Charles C., 12, 128
Johns Hopkins University, 69
journals. *See* periodicals
juvenile books. *See* children's books

lectern-system library, 20, 22, 24, 30, 61
lending. *See* circulation
Library of Congress, 9, 10, 11–12, 106, 128
Library of Congress Classification System, 46, 48, 85, 86
library services by fax machine, 9
library services by mail, 8–9
library services by telephone, 9
library services by teletype machine, 9
lighting, in libraries, 8, 23, 24, 27, 29, 88
Lincoln Cathedral (England), library, 26

Macdonald, Angus Snead, 29
McGill University, library, 136
McKin, Charles Follen, 28
magazines. *See* periodicals
management theories, 4–5
MARC, 12, 128
Mesopotamian libraries, 15, 16, 33–4, 124
    catalog, 34
microfiches. *See* microforms
microfilms. *See* microforms

microforms, 12, 49, 71
Minneapolis Free Public Library, 67, 68
misplacement, 66, 75, 83
modular-design libraries. *See* open-plan libraries
monastery libraries, 19, 20, 21, 23, 25, 30, 36–8, 55, 58, 60, 72, 124, 126
 lending of books, 59–60, 72, 124
 See also under specific monasteries

Naudé, Gabriel, 39, 40, 63, 127
New York Mercantile Library catalog, 128
New York Public Library, 10, 49
newspaper room, 65
 See also browsing areas and rooms
Nineveh, library of, 15, 34, 57
Nippur, library of, 15, 125
nonfiction books, 10, 49, 50, 51, 52, 53, 93, 111, 113
novels. *See* fiction books

OCLC. *See* Online Computer Library Center
Online Computer Library Center (OCLC), 9
Online Public Access Catalog (OPAC), 87, 105, 134, 136
OPAC. *See* Online Public Access Catalog
open-shelf system, 28, 31, 45, 46, 47, 56, 57, 61–2, 65, 66, 67, 68–9, 70, 71, 75, 83, 87, 88, 108, 118, 120
open-plan libraries, 28, 29, 31
open stacks. *See* open-shelf system
Ottoman libraries, 62
Oxford University, libraries, 22, 23, 24, 25, 61, 62, 127, 129
 See also Bodleian Library

palace libraries, 33, 34, 55
Palatine library, 58
 See also Roman libraries
Panizzi, Anthony, 44, 128
papyrus, 10, 11, 12, 16, 17, 30, 55, 72
paper, 10, 11, 12, 20
parchment, 10, 11, 12, 16–17, 30
Pergamon library, 17

periodicals, 49, 67, 70, 93, 95, 97, 104, 105, 106, 131–2, 137
Pinakes, 35, 55, 125
photocopy machine, 10
Poole, William F., 45–6
presses. *See* armaria (presses)
printing, 7, 11, 25, 130
public libraries, 28, 48, 49–51, 52, 53, 54, 58, 60, 64, 66, 68, 73, 97
 access to the collection, 68–9, 71, 79, 88
 and browsing, 88, 97, 98, 110–14, 117, 119–20, 136
 services to children, 49–50
 services to elderly, 50–1
 services to young-adults, 50
 See also under specific public libraries
Putnam, Herbert, 67, 68
Ranganathan, S. R., 48, 71, 86
reading rooms and areas. *See* browsing rooms and areas

Richardson, Henry Hobson, 27–8
Roman libraries, 18–19, 36, 55, 57, 58, 124
Rullmann, F., 44

Sainte-Geneviève Abbey, library of, 26, 28, 42–3, 63
Saint-Germain-des-Prés, library of, 26, 59
Saint Martin's Priory of Dover, library of, 37
 catalog, 12, 37, 126–7
Saint Victor (Paris), library of, 36–7, 59
 catalog, 37
shelves and shelving, browsing among. *See* browsing, among the shelves
 as storage medium, 16, 18, 19, 20, 24, 25, 26, 27, 28, 29, 30, 36, 37, 43, 44, 45–6, 47, 49, 51, 61, 63, 65, 66, 68, 71–2, 73, 75, 78, 79, 82, 89, 111, 124, 125, 135, 136
Sion College Library, 41
Sorbonne University, library, 39, 60, 61, 62, 63
 catalog, 39